SOM
journal

2

Hatje Cantz

Contents

Introduction
Integrity

SOM's project to conduct a series of external criticisms of current work has met with a variety of responses outside SOM itself. In the general media, the opening of one of the world's largest practices to critical, external eyes has been described by one journal as a "courageous" approach (*ArchNewsNow*, April 16, 2002) and by another as an attempt at a "more objective assessment" (*New York Times*, September 29, 2002). Free from the influence of those assessed, the resulting publication is seen to be different from the more normal "self-congratulatory monographs" *(NYT)*.

Among architects, reactions have been more mixed, ranging from the unquotable to that of grudging respect. Certainly this form of external review has charted new territory, casting other practice profiles in a more critical light, or, to quote Fred Bernstein from the *New York Times,* "makes a typical architecture firm's monograph read like a high school yearbook."

Just over a year after the first adjudication of current SOM projects by external critics had taken place in New York, a new jury of five individuals convened on June 10, 2002, at the Chicago office of SOM. This time the selection panel consisted of the architect and critic Doug Garofalo (Chicago), the structural engineer Werner Sobek (Stuttgart), the artist James Turrell (Flagstaff), the architect and critic Wilfried Wang (Berlin), and the architect Tod Williams (New York).

Following the intense debate within SOM since the results of the first selection had become known *(SOM Journal 1),* the original intention to maintain the jury for the second round was dropped. It was a decision made by the Chicago-based partners of SOM in response to the concern that the first set of jurors (three out of five from New York) might have been too close to the issues developed at the New York office. Since concerns of partiality often cross competitors' minds, and despite the participating jurors' insistence that they did not know the origin of the submitted projects, a newly composed jury reassured the doubters of the independence of the selection process.

As in the first event, a majority of projects that were selected originated in the New York office (six out of nine). While this question might not interest the reader outside the world of SOM, it goes without saying that the repeated success of the New York office is further intensifying internal debates.

The *Journal* might thus become a source of reflection on central questions facing any practice. How does one achieve a high degree of quality in design in the face of an often limited interest and capacity on behalf of client bodies in this aspect? How can a project synthesize the advancement of legitimate client interests as well as long-term issues of programmatic, aesthetic, and material durability? How can a claim be made for architecture to have a wider socio-cultural relevance beyond spectacle or speculation?

The selection process followed the pattern of the first occasion. The jurors individually spent a good part of the morning digesting each one of the sixty-two submitted schemes. Subsequently selection criteria were loosely debated, which, in the course of the day, became increasingly explicit, as the reader of the jury transcripts will find.

A first tour around the displayed work was undertaken, in which any project that did not receive even one vote was eliminated. Thirty-eight schemes were thus removed. A further fifteen were voted out during the second round. Nine schemes were left. A brief, but intense discussion on the option of reducing the number of schemes even further did not find common ground, so that despite reservations here and there, the nine finalists were ultimately chosen for publication.

The jurors' comments were occasionally enthusiastic, sometimes damning; sentiments ranged from respect to incredulity. Some of the jurors openly acknowledged that they had learned a lot from the review. Some had changed their view of SOM. One of the greatest impressions was made by a scheme from the "traditional" field of expertise (the office and high-rises) as well as by schemes from the "unexpected" field of small-scale projects. Conceptual innovations were seen in the case of the Mega Tower as well as in the various school projects. Unanimity, or a state of mind close to it, was recorded in these instances.

There was also unanimity on the criticism of the frequent lack of concise and precise descriptions, a state of affairs previously noted by Jenny Holzer of the first jury. Too often architects leave the written discourse to the last moment. This may be either due to the fact that architects prefer to express their ideas in anything else but written form, or due to the fact that they believe it to be a relatively easy task, given their acquaintance with the scheme over the intense design period. However, the lack of clarity often found in these descriptive texts more often results from the lack of clarity that evidently exists between ideas and designs, the written document simply revealing that state of affairs.

Were architects more self-critical—and this does not solely apply to those designers who submitted schemes to the *SOM Journal 2* jury—a period of close reflection on the factual achievement in relation to the expressed idea would benefit both: the design and the text.

The jury acknowledged the effort that SOM is undertaking in the field of environmental systems. The establishment of an analytical support group able to evaluate the impact of designs across the practice regarding their resource consumption and ability to recycle these was welcomed. However, given the extensive research that is being undertaken in this field both by architects such Thomas Herzog (Munich) or systematic analysts such as Niklaus Kohler (Karlsruhe), SOM's own environmental group was seen as adequate in the general context, but insufficient in terms of the leadership role to which SOM would be expected to aspire.

The "end game" debate among the jurors focused on the issue of design integrity of large architectural practices, the role of research as one basis for the establishment of such integrity, and the need to develop a common design attitude. Werner Sobek, who took the lead in this discussion, made it clear that he was not looking for an office style, but for a communality of values regarding the practice's direction.

Can there be common values in a large practice on how given programs are interpreted in a broader manner, exceeding the client's expectations? Can a large practice develop principles on the basis of these values that determine the use of materials, the implementation of structure, the addressing of environmental issues, and ultimately the creation of communal symbols? In short: can a practice define architecture's task beyond its instrumental boundary of the material, functional, or financial to incorporate broader roles of constructing a cultured environment? The aspect of integrity as it relates to a design itself (and its relation to the material world), to the design team (including the client and the authorities), and to the process of its realization can be scrutinized with some descriptive precision. The other aspect of integrity, that of the relation between a design concept and its cultural and ethical con-

text, is more open to debate. These two aspects will be further developed following the discussion of the nine selected projects, as well as the body of work that is now beginning to constitute itself when seen together with the six schemes of *SOM Journal 1*.

Nine of the Best

One private house, two items of infrastructure, two cultural projects, three schools, and a high-rise tower were selected. Not a typical cross-section, one might think, for the kind of work with which SOM has been associated in the past. Two of them had unanimous support, two received four out of the five possible votes, and the other five had a majority of jurors behind them. Even so, each of these, if and when completed, would command the attention of any architect. Some of the objections were based on the lack of the scheme's clarity, its inconsistency between stated intentions and actual design, other objections related to fundamental opposition to a project's premise, be it the structural or the siting concept.

In some respects, this selection raises a question for SOM, as only one scheme was chosen by the jury from the building type (the office) to which SOM's reputation is conventionally tied. To be sure, the office building has been and still is the mainstay of SOM's production. A large part of the submissions consisted of designs for speculative offices or, at any rate, proposals that included a large component of office use. Only one of these could convince the jury: the skyscraper for Beijing, called the Mega Tower. In the penultimate round, a quarter of the total number of submitted schemes belonged to this building type. Three of these were close to reaching a majority (Fulton Street, TI Tower, CCTV Headquarters). In comparison with the first jury, when two out of the five selected schemes were office buildings, the results of the second jury will send the SOM partners back thinking.

The Marina Bay Bank Headquarters project *(SOM Journal 1)* used a flexible section to permit not only variable leases but also different office types, all of which were to be brought in contact with occasional garden terraces. The 350 Madison Avenue office addition *(SOM Journal 1)* was seen as a bold urban intervention, not merely as an opportunistic densification of an already intensely used part of New York City. The perennial debate about extension and architectural language, about conservation issues, was here resolved using a self-conscious juxtaposition with the subtle absorption of elements of the existing in the projected new.

The office schemes submitted to *SOM Journal 2* appeared to pursue one or the other preparatory research. In most cases there was insufficient logical strength between the research and the result. The Canary Wharf office block being a typical case in point: here the open research on atria locations and sizes disappointingly gave birth to the conventional solution. A second quasi-research project, Redefining the Suburban Office Park, began on a strong premise in its fundamental critique only to render a grass-covered version of the normative approach.

The Mega Tower for Beijing brings together a view of urban life in a high-rise development which might help to reduce the monofunctional nature of office districts. In incorporating a large hotel within its central volume, the Mega Tower becomes an urban node for a large public beyond the sole service sector users. The way this mixed program is accommodated in the layered tower is in tune with the structural concept that draws on the structural behavior of the bamboo culm or stem.

Refining and adapting this structural analogy for the purposes of a high-rise convinced the jury at once. Particularly the dilating space between inner and

outer structure fascinated the reviewers. Coming within the well-established considerations on double glass skin envelopes, this high-rise design synthesizes a number of current considerations, while forming yet another link to the heroic era of SOM's own high-rise designs of the 1970s. In accepting the potential of non-orthogonal design for the perimeter frame—triangulation in its variety of possibilities (a route from Eugene Viollet-le-Duc, Anne Tyng, and Louis Kahn, to Fazlur Khan)—the Mega Tower is a form that expresses its constitution, a modernist tradition.

The two large infrastructural projects included in *SOM Journal 1,* New York's Pennsylvania Station and Singapore's Changi International Airport Terminal, represent the character of contemporary infrastructure commissions. Rather than constructing entirely new figures on a green field or within a city, the turn of the millennium has seen the adaptation and reconfiguration of existing facilities. Airports, railway stations, nodes of modal interchange have been the focus of secondary and tertiary transport system grafts. In this sense, the Dulles Airport People Mover, selected for this *Journal,* has had to demonstrate a respect for the old while at the same time subtly overcoming the latter's shortfalls. Here, not merely the technical difficulties have had to be overcome, but within the melee of conditions, public safety aspects, even conservation issues, the

 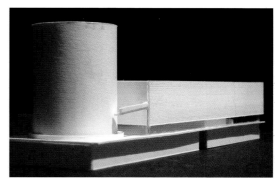

architects have had to hold up the identity of the new sediment.

The Dulles Airport Automated People Mover System (APMS) allows for the replacement of the mobile lounges while the operability of the airport is maintained. Daylighting of the underground level is achieved by constructing a lattice-like beam system which grafts onto the striking Saarinen roof structure. Thus, as a user, one does not have a sense that the APMS is not an incompatible addition, but that it is in every sense of the word an organic extension.

The Central Plant at the University of California Merced, which generally speaking might be included in this category of infrastructure, is programmatically more a piece of equipment of technology than a building used by a segment of the public. Its role is that of a symbolic node on campus with the theme of resource provision. In the context of a new campus the Central Plant is to be seen and admired (at night) and not heard (given the extensive efforts at insulating it in acoustic terms).

The designers intended the configuration to relate to the agricultural silos of the Central Valley. At night, partial views of the inner organism would be revealed through selected lighting and the shrouding of different layers with the outermost one consisting of perforated aluminum. A normative program element of a large institution is thus treated with care, giving the potential of a building becoming an understandable, yet also ethereal object.

Unusual for SOM's normal scope of work, the jury selected a single family dwelling for inclusion in *Journal 2.* The scheme, Jordan House outside Lisbon, Portugal, was discussed not without controversy. The supporters saw in it the potential for developing elegant, even beautiful sculptural forms. Given the advancements in 3D software, the particular curvatures of the complex, yet compelling roof form would be easily realizable. However, the detractors of the scheme saw in the mixture of patinated copper sheet and timber structural frame a curious choice of constructional detailing that runs counter to the expectations raised in the streamlined form. Given the sophisticated modeling software, a structure and detailing more akin to the stressed skin or monocoque system would have been more apt.

Added to this criticism was the charge that the spatial composition had more to do with a Palladian villa than a streamlined or futuristically styled figure. The roof as something quite apart from anything else was seen by the detractors as an add-on, not as an organic part of the potentially interesting house.

In contrast to the Kuwait Police College, included in *SOM Journal 1,* which is a vocational training institution, the spate of schools and colleges selected for *SOM Journal 2* fulfils more closely the expectations of an educational institution. The strength of their presence among the finalists impressed the entire jury. Especially Elementary School Number 11 in Fairfield, Connecticut, elicited reactions of surprise, given the tight budget of such commissions and the resulting relatively small fee. Jurors queried SOM's ability to provide the usual comprehensive service, for which it is known, at best at cost for this elementary school.

The resolution of the plan with its combination of repetitive classrooms and kidney-shaped spaces provides as much memorable circulation domains as it retains something of the innocence of the left-over, conserved trees. Opposing geometries—orthogonal exterior versus kidney-shaped special volumes—emphasize the continuous relation between nature and artifice, the presence of one in the other.

Concentration on essential constructional elements, such as special concrete blocks for the exterior walls and glazing bars, helps in the realization of such an ambitious building. The rigorous translation of an appropriate concept via minimal details to achieve a rich architecture has been the primary purpose of architects' inventiveness, here it has every chance of becoming reality.

In a more intense relation between site and architecture, the New Upper School and Library at the Greenwich Academy in Greenwich, Connecticut, weaves together two distinct topographies with a 23-foot difference. Thus it is the building with its four departments and related light wells which forms the node. The architecture is a porous translator of the two levels, allowing movement, program, and light to merge.

James Turrell, who refrained from voting on this scheme, collaborated on the four light chambers, which each consist of a timber framing system that incorporates colored strip lights in the purlins. The specific weighting of the three basic color components of white gives each chamber a distinct atmos-

phere. Using its extensive space planning experience, SOM was able to bring to the commission tight program control with its intended flexibilities as well as the unique contribution of Turrell's light sensibility, that ensures a subtle characterization of each light box in relation to the respective academic department.

Similar to Turrell's contribution to the Kuwait Police College, the Greenwich Academy benefits from the artist's effortless architectural thinking in light. In the New Upper School and Library, SOM transforms conventional and inexpensive building components into an architecture specific to its site. No longer is there a reliance on motifs and stylistic elements so commonly seen in postmodernist designs; instead, the school is an exploration in basic architectural alchemy.

The third educational institution that was selected for publication was the Deerfield Science, Mathematics, and Technology Center in Deerfield, Connecticut. Once again too, the involvement of James Turrell in the most ambitious design of the three school buildings has introduced light as an interpretive medium for the building's presence on the site. The new building's changing relationship to time and thus to the seasons ultimately leads to the realization that these gradually evolving phenomena, that science, mathematics, and technology constitute their own discernable disciplines within this building in particular. Frame, activity, and human observation within these are explored in this design.

The jury, on this occasion extensively coached by Turrell, who again refrained from voting on the scheme, did not have to be convinced by the design's ambitions, but was more skeptical regarding the detailed success of the design. Much will depend on the widely used glazing within the floor and wall construction, much will also depend on the truly traversable grassed roof terraces, which, like the Greenwich Academy New Upper School, negotiate the change in level on either side of the SMT Center.

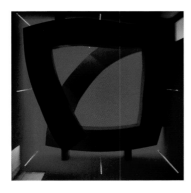

Deerfield SMT Center is one of the most comprehensive efforts at involving the corpus of the building's users—science teachers and experts from
fields within the subjects that are to be taught and
experienced within the building—that is known in
recent architecture. SOM's ability to draw these
experts to the design table owes as much to its
ambitions as to its experience in managing such
complex collaborations.

While the Kuwait Police College reveals almost
an autistic logic to its composition, the Deerfield
SMT Center shows an architectural syntax evolved
from the program's immediately related phenomena.
The building has the potential to use these phenomena as instruments for articulating human experiences and for the positioning of individual as well
as collective consciousness in the subject of science at large and in the particular object of the
institution. In its intention to go beyond the known
astronomical architectures, the building is taking
a large risk.

A category of building types not present in *SOM
Journal 1* is that for culture. One year ago, the
Beijing City Museum just missed being included in
the final round. A cathedral design was eliminated
in the second round. This year, two projects have
been included: the competition entry for Avery
Fisher Hall in New York and the Visitor Center at the

base of the Washington Monument. Both schemes
were closely confined by pre-existing conditions:
in New York it was the urban setting which pre-
scribed a certain volume for a replacement concert
hall, in Washington it was the existing obelisk that
was to be augmented by an underground exhibition
space.

The monumental base—a mixture of architecture
and landscaping consisting of three sedimented cir-
cular and elliptical planes, some set an angle to
each other—forms an extensive and proportionately
commensurate plinth to the enormous obelisk. At
night, the resultant dynamism of the visual interre-
lation of the illuminated retaining walls would create
a sublime atmosphere, befitting for a contemporary
revaluation of an ancient form. The jury was less
taken by the layout of the visitor center itself, particularly the curvilinear partitions, that seem to
weaken the boldness of the inclined circles and
ellipses; it was also unconvinced by the actual
entrance, a vomitorium-type opening to the side of
the base ellipse. The design's strength resides in
the limpid interplay of inclined round planes and
their nighttime light effect.

Similar is the Avery Fisher Hall proposal: this
scheme owes its magic to the contrasting condition
provided by darkness. The interior comes to life and
the inner light brings the glass and translucent
stone panels to radiate beyond its physical cur-

tilage. The building is ingeniously thought of as a web of three-dimensional vierendeels. Alone this fact allows for the monumental cantilevers, which exude a gravity that can only be described as awe-inspiring. The theme of light drama is continued on the inside in the manner in which the orchestra, the artists' entry onto the stage, the auditorium's boxes and balconies are accentuated and framed. Here, of course, the inspiration from the Beinecke Library at Yale (Gordon Bunshaft of SOM, 1963), itself dramatic in its spatial and structural qualities, is furthered to a level of daring and phenomenal excess, that must have raised eyebrows of concerned skepticism among the Avery Fisher Hall jury.

The competition entry by SOM leaves much unspoken, there is no indication of a structural concept, there are no details of staging and acoustics. All the jury saw were images of the models and their insertion in a photoshopped context. Yet, the fascination of the visual promise was such that it convinced a majority of the jury.

Integrity: Beyond Self-Sufficient Consistency

As a whole, the nine schemes each had powerful ideas at the root of their form, even if some of them were less well developed. In this context, the issue of the inner coherence of a scheme, the relation between the conceptual promise to its representational manifestation, could be said to be the architects' quintessential realm of intellectual expression, the realm in which the design needs to have its convincing and compelling arguments rooted. The inner coherence is but another expression for integrity between concept and architectural form.

Beyond these basic internal relations, however, an architectural design expresses values that concern not only the fulfillment of a program, but consciously or not, it is both active in the making of a reality as well as in the expression of such values. Thus, for instance, the never-ending competition for the tallest building is part of a value system that presupposes the boundless abilities of technology and the need to harness this for the purposes of gaining a symbolic hegemony over any previous holder of such a title. The belief in the limitless nature of technology, of human artifice, is an expression of the value in which certain individuals see themselves. The technology required for such a high-rise may not be explicitly represented; however, its presence is a prerequisite for the simple fact of the tower's existence. Technology, or for that matter any other con-

tributory or constitutive aspect of the building's physical presence, does not have to be consciously or expressly represented for that aspect to be interpretable as part of the design's overall belief system.

The two kinds of integrity of an architectural design, the inner coherence between design concept and architectural form and the expression of the values upon which the design is based, can be traced back to the design's morphology. Thus when seen against the foil of existing conditions, a building's formal and spatial constitution can be read as an index of the architects' response to that existing condition as well as their attempt at its reshaping. In every building design, therefore, there exists an acceptance of a given reality as well as a desire to change it. There are of course different degrees of acceptance and of desires for change, which can be deduced by comparing the design to the standard solutions in a similar physical and cultural context.

In the cultural context of resource efficiency, those designs that seek to change the hitherto normal rate of consumption of material and energy resources would therefore be seen as attempts at changing the status quo. Such an attitude could be compared to a design's physical constitution, including its contextual emplacement, but would not necessarily be compared to its formal representation,

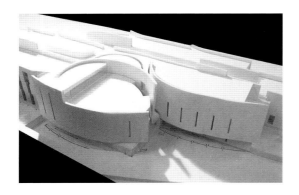 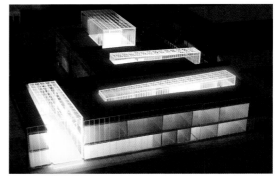

given the many ways of constructing and completing a building's envelope.

A building's siting is one of the most powerful modes of expressing the cultural values of the designers. In seeking to merge a building's configuration with the site's character, as seen in the case of the Greenwich Academy and Deerfield SMT Center, the architects are putting an end to object fetishism. The architects achieve this by mimetically replacing the existing changes in the sites through the buildings' own outer forms. While this siting strategy may neither significantly reduce the rate of resource consumption of either institution nor be an imposition on the site that would be easily reversible, the two designs represent a different attitude to the conventional approach. Coupled with a conscious attempt at reducing resource consumption both in construction and in use, the two designs could be comprehensive examples of a new direction for building practice, particularly in the USA.

Beyond the design of the individual building, there are medium-sized issues such as constructing on the periphery of settlements (for instance, SOM's project for Redefining the Suburban Office Park) and the very large scale of design: urban and regional planning. In this regard, the Chicago Central Area Plan, which was developed by SOM and which integrated other schemes that SOM had

been designing, appeared less ambitious in its environmental concerns. The Chicago Central Area Plan included a comprehensive redevelopment of the Lake Shore, but remained timid in regard to the future of the river embankments. While the jury had no information on the scope of the commission for the plan, it appeared to be a traditional zoning and density study. The environmental impact of future high-rises, the effect of the continued development within the Loop and its environs on transport, and the micro-climatic changes as a result of these developments seemed to the jurors to be still in need of investigation. Given SOM's establishment of an environmental advisory group, such knowledge and experience would have been of benefit to the Chicago Central Area Plan.

SOM's projects give evidence of their ability to manage complex projects with the involvement of numerous client representatives and user groups, not to mention funding authorities and building control representatives. The Deerfield SMT Center is perhaps the most outstanding example of the way that different interests have been brought together. The resultant design, were it successful in its formal, material, and phenomenal intentions, would constitute a high degree of integrity: formal, ethical, and experiential. In their daily and seasonal use, the students of the center would become aware of the building's siting and situation, a situation that goes beyond its geographical and institutional position and that embraces architecture's ability to become a medium for the transformation of the users' awareness.

The Deerfield SMT Center could therefore become a paradigm case for SOM's sense of responsibility that such an understanding of integrity brings. An architectural or urban design commission will only make an improvement beyond its immediate context, if the practice that is charged with such a commission divests its responsibility to the best of its knowledge and experience. The Deerfield SMT Center did not have to be as complex as it is in SOM's design. A few normal classrooms in concrete boxes would have sufficed. However, client, users and architects seemed to have recognized the opportunity to propose a scheme that goes well beyond the normal frame of reference.

Divesting an architectural practice's responsibility to the best of its knowledge and experience may well mean that a design proposal exceeds the needs and expectations (and partial interests) of the client. With the ever-increasing scope of issues that architects have to confront, the knowledge base and the range of experiences may appear to become unmanageable. Nevertheless, there appear to be principles which practices can develop, which begin to guide a path through the wealth of issues, and which have greater goals in mind than either the reductive satisfaction of a program or the mere fulfillment of formalist desires. These principles would be defined in relation to the aspirations that a practice has vis-à-vis contributing towards a cultured environment. It is not within the remit of a jury member or an editor of such a publication to determine these for any practice (other than her or his own), however the review of the selected schemes in this publication describes values, principles, and instances of designs.

Architects have been and continue to be in the thick of many fields: legal, industrial, material, social, economic, ecological, formal, spatial, symbolic. Most of these fields have been occupied by experts whose educational background does not lie in architecture. Yet it is still the architect, whether working in a small or large practice, who is able to be the arbiter of these diverse interests. The ability to make such a voice of informed arbitration heard, to direct the practice's knowledge and experience to goals beyond the practice's own interests, to bring all participants in a building project to the same intent, to withstand the daily grinding, all these qualities contribute to the practice's authoritative standing.

The integrity of an architectural practice lies therefore in this: to design with the concerns of a wider population in mind, to propose edifices whose symbolic and material voices may be heard well beyond our own lifetimes, to give cause for both reflection and inspiration through building cultured environments.

Wilfried Wang, Berlin—Austin, October 2002

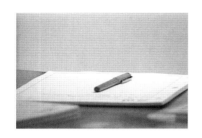  

Jury Transcript

Wilfried Wang, Douglas Garofalo, Werner Sobek, James Turrell, and Tod Williams
June 8, 2002
224 South Michigan Avenue, Chicago

Wilfried Wang Where should we begin?

James Turrell Let's start in the corner by the door...

WW The police station in New York City, accommodating the Central Command and also the central location for 911 telephone calls. This design is based on the idea of weaponry, camouflage.

JT The scheme is interesting in the way the concept is represented, its references are appealing, but I really don't find these expressed in the building.

Tod Wiliams No, not at all—it's just a very superficial area in the front and doesn't change the plan, the expression, or the experience of the building.

WW What I find particularly disconcerting is the lack of relationship between the spatial organization of the interior and the exterior form. The idea of radiating with such a powerful form is in no way reflected on the interior, so that the exterior is literally cladding without any intellectual rigor to it.

Werner Sobek I would not vote for it.

JT I had a vote for it, given the research. It's handsomely presented and interesting.

Douglas Garofalo But it's suspect.

TW But the problem is that possibly one person did the research and another person the design.

DG Maybe it was an older person doing the research and the younger person the design.

TW That's the better way to say it.

WW Had we not had this drawing, I think we would be quite intrigued.

JT Actually in the stealth aircraft image there is a good representation of exactly where we are. This is a revolutionary aircraft that can hardly fly. In fact, it can't fly without a computer, and its only mission is to get in without being seen by radar. So it's made for that totally, and it has nothing to do with aerodynamics. Those are the interesting issues: how we're going to have to camouflage, what role does the police have in society, but I don't find that excitingly expressed in the stratification of the site.

WS That's the point.

JT It's just preposterous to even see the stealth bomber flying, but, boy, it's effective. There will be those things in architecture I am sure...

WW The next scheme is the Central Plant at UC Merced.

JT I like this building—it's just what it is, we need those things around us, and we need to have them made well, it's a triumph for what we need to do in the industrial parts of our lives.

TW I totally agree, I was more intrigued

by this structure, but I suppose they are just louvers, is that correct? They are just big windbreakers.

JT They have to do with this cooling tower.

TW The building is simple and direct, no nonsense.

JT Doing something as well as this is impressive, I vote for it.

WW OK, so that stays in.

JT So, we are on to the next scheme...

WW Jordan House.

JT I was pleased, I am interested in this scheme.

DG I am too. It's a pure bombast actually. It's a relief after the other things on the wall.

JT Graphically it's so well done.

DG Yes, so well done.

TW I would like to have had a section here.

JT We have something of an elevation there.

DG I'd wish the plan didn't revert back to this mode of centralization—you'd think with a form like this you would have a different sense of the interior planning.

WW The plan is its undoing.

JT I'm interested in the project.

WS OK, we keep that.

WW Alright, 300 Madison Avenue, New

York City. Here's one of those many attempts to deal with the conventional office block and how to make it more interesting. In this case Bridget Riley is being quoted—it's one of two schemes that refers to artwork and then reapplies the principles to the development of cladding surfaces.

DG I want to believe it, but I got down to here, and I just wonder what happens to it?

WW Or you get down to there, and then you wonder.

JT There are a number of projects of patterning that are fairly interesting in intent, though you don't see the payoff.

WW Once again, the background research and the concepts are interesting and compelling, but they don't penetrate further than the skins.

TW I can definitely see that it's an un-

doing, but why one wouldn't one include that? I think that the research on what can be done to the skin of a building is interesting itself. But, again, I don't even see that it's paying off here.

JT One of the criticisms I noticed in the last *Journal* was just the same discussion on the lack of description of what the architects are charged with, what they are actually doing. That doesn't seem to have been read by this year's participants. Just a little bit more of contextual description would help.

TW I think that's true.

WW Well, as Kenneth Frampton said last time, and it's also true this time, it's that monstrous logic of the New York real-estate market which reduces the freedom that the architect has to an absolute minimum, and this is in a way an expression of that condition.

JT This is also done in Berlin where many of the buildings are required to be clad in stone.

WW In Berlin it's a building regulation, a local idiosyncrasy. Here the discussion revolves around maximum floor area to minimum envelope, and so on.

JT Well, just like the fascist regulations they have in Santa Fe, where everything has to be either territorial or Pueblo style, and there are a lot of other places that are doing that, not to mention how many designs are driven by ADA nowadays.

WS Yet, in a lot of cases such regulations are necessary.

JT Yes.

WS I don't think there is any excuse for that . . .

WW All right, so here we are with the Deerfield Science and Math Technology Center.

DG I actually have a vote for this one. I think it's underdeveloped, still a bit crude, but I really like its concept. I think it's a good response.

JT I have to be honest with this one, I have worked on this project. I want to say how much we worked with the astronomer to bring events into different rooms at different times of the year.

DG Into that brick network?

JT Yes, different patterns of the year into the brick network.

TW And it's not even represented.

JT This man from the Naval Observatory has spent nearly a year working with me on all of the different lighting events that come down through sometimes two and

three rooms, to get at it, and I don't see any of it here.

TW I don't either.

DG I support it as a strategy. I don't think it's very clearly described.

JT They are doing an interesting job as far as siting is concerned, bringing together the lawns at different levels, something which you don't see either. My criticism here is directed at the presentation; they could do a better job of expressing what the project is.

TW I thought this was a weird quote: "How can we make a building that doesn't reveal itself over time."

JT That's one of the supporters, a trustee.

TW I see, but wouldn't you say, "How can we make a building that does reveal itself over time?"

JT I think it will be more the latter if it does, but it has different things happening nearly every day. Sort of on a mirror image . . .

TW The presentation needs another section here.

WW You are right, James, I think there is not enough information here to really support it.

JT Some of the issues of time and light that were worked on are not shown here.

TW This seems an impenetrable wall and not porous or layered.

JT It runs along these lines and down on to it, but you don't see it in the presentation.

TW So am I inside or outside the building?

JT You are outside.

JT So on the outside one can walk along on the top of the building all the way down.

WS It's not possible to understand this quality when you stand in front of the building, this elevation doesn't show anything about these stepping-down lawns.

TW Because the building is conceptually a retaining wall, but what is it retaining?

It doesn't feel like a retaining wall because it is running parallel. You don't sense a lateral force.

WS So we keep it in . . . Next, the public school, Elementary School Number 11.

TW I appreciate the modest approach.

JT It's a modest thing. If that were to have been my elementary school it would have been terrific.

TW I agree although it's not a particularly new idea, but if it could be built, I would be happy to experience it.

DG Yes, I agree.

WW OK that's clear enough . . . Here we have a group that is involved in analyzing the energy efficiency of different designs and their components. There's a lot of text here, which I haven't read at all.

WS I haven't either.

JT Me neither. You won't read that before lunch.

TW We didn't read it as it doesn't engage our attention—it's not well presented.

JT Who's read it?

TW No, I read a sentence or two. I just kept looking at those stamp-sized images and thought about how I don't ever want to do energy-efficient design, when you see that it makes someone just trying to obey the standards of the book rather than to transcend them.

WW The problem with this is that there are so many different aspects to energy-efficient design: the building's components, the building in use, the building's orientation, etc. It's impossible to summarize on a single page what you have analyzed and what you would like to analyze, and how you have actually proven its energy efficiency—so a lot of this has to be taken on trust.

JT Does the same thing apply to the great green buildings? I always ask architects this question, and it's a fair question to ask. Name the great green buildings.

DG I think there's Werner's house. It's a zero-energy building.

JT Really?

WS Yes, my house is a zero-energy building. These are important issues, and it's important to pursue them and to have them done well. There are many green buildings, and there are even zero-energy buildings, some that even feed electricity back into mains. It's important how these issues are incorporated into everyday design.

DG You don't get architecture automatically from a zero-energy building.

WW This is more a question of the establishment of an SOM environmental services group supervising or looking into some of these aspects. That's the important issue.

JT It is important.

WW I would say this is what one should expect to find in any office.

TW The presentation doesn't say that it not only did the work responsibly, but

that it transcends the prescriptive requirements of the codes. That's the only aspect that interests me: to what extent does it transcend the manual?

DG Is this an organization within SOM that evaluates all of the buildings—is it newly formed, is it a new research arm within the constellation of the firm? If it were some setup as such that we could grab on to and say: well, here's an effort in this area with a good deal of intellect and capital behind it. But it does look like it's just: here's how we evaluate these buildings in the design process. That's what we all do.

WS Frankly, I haven't read it in total, but I have the feeling in order to be fair that someone should read it and then report to the jury.

DG If you agree, I would be ready to do this. Environmental aspects are very important, and I think we should support this especially in the American building market.

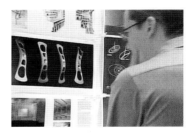

WW OK. Next, this is the Memorial Sloan Kettering Research Lab. It's an addition to an existing facility, a high-rise component with a laboratory on one side and offices on the other.

DG It looks comprehensively done, but I can't get excited about it.

TW One of the things that I have been learning a little about is laboratory planning, but I don't see anything extraordinary. I did look a little at the plans, and it's more than competent. But this is a tight site. I think it's quite a good job, but again I won't say it is transcendent.

WW The presentation is one of the best we have seen in terms of the day and night contexts. It then reveals the details.

JT If you have a vote for it, leave it in...

TW I voted for this next one.

WW The Mega Tower in Beijing.

WS Maybe we should discuss it in detail.

WS I am sure there are some misleading concepts here, but I think this should not be the reason to throw it out.

JT I was interested in this Mega Tower. Who is interested in this design? I like the form within the form, so let's discuss this.

TW I like the design, independent of the bamboo concept.

DG I think that's the first one we are unanimous on. It was an easy pick for me too.

WW So it's in, let's move on...

JT Let's look at the Chicago Redevelopment Plan. I just want to say that this redevelopment is a little hard for me—but boy is it ever needed—just like the green principles are needed, but how do we go about doing it?

TW Well, this had that exact same wall of information that was so hard to get past, so I'd be happy to sit down and look at it more carefully.

JT One of us should.

WW I wouldn't say that I looked at it in detail. It makes the point that the large-scale interventions of the sixties were an error. This design proposes to return to the smaller grain of earlier times, around 1940, introducing some larger green spaces in relation to recreation

and civic spaces. I believe that this is the right way to go, I am less taken by these houses here, but as a type they are OK. These are four-to five-story apartment buildings with shops at ground level.

TW Really?

JT This site is very close to IIT.

TW This could have been more interesting. Again, I haven't looked at it closely, but I would have been more interested if they said what happened in the sixties wasn't that great, but we can make it better. Accept the problem and develop from it, rather than return to something old.

WW Right. That's another option which some architects have investigated elsewhere. But I don't think that's the option in this case as these high-rises are just being knocked down.

JT As we speak.

TW Are all of them being knocked down?

DG All of them?

WW They have been so tainted in their use that even that kind of reform is no longer possible.

JT Lost mystique.

TW What bothers me is that this seems it's neither here nor there.

WW Well, I would vote for this.

TW OK, I will take another look at it.

WS Sorry, here somebody is working really hard to make these areas more dense, to get more people to live here, and at the same time to have more of green space as well as a higher quality of living. All of this is very pos-itive, but must it end in an architecture like this?

WW No it doesn't, this is probably not going to be included in the publication. I think of it as research.

WW The Hotel Sofitel in San Francisco. Will this withstand an earthquake?

JT They won't get it built if they can't engineer it. The design has a sort of a genuflect to it.

DG Sort of a knee bend.

WW It has a certain elegance to it.

DG Stylish, that's what the program is.

JT I am able to consider it again.

WW OK, we will take it into the next round.

TW I must say that it is so stylish on the outside that I expected it to be different on the inside.

DG Well, you are just used to those computer renderings.

WW It's a typical case of where the hotel likes the modern expression on the exterior, but prefers the Louis XIV within.

JT And Sofitel is like that. It's true...

WW OK. The Carpet Tiles Project: SOM-Milliken.

JT While I could get into carpet tiles, I basically wouldn't want to. I was excited to think that carpet tiles were an entire project.

WW It's a beginning, you can see that at the end of the presentation they are finally exploring color.

DG I had this one on my list, because as soon as they started talking about ink-jet printers and being able to do what you can do with a printer, I thought that's good use of technology.

TW I totally agree. I also had this one on my list, but then I don't see what the technology is doing and what the innovation is.

WW I think it's worth keeping.

DG There are a lot of very compelling things in this.

JT You would be having your students doing that, wouldn't you?

WW OK, so this is in for now...

WW Chicago Central Area Plan.

DG I had marked this one, but I have a question about SOM's role. I am familiar with the 2020 plan which was drafted by the municipal society. Are these just illustrations for the plan, or is there more to it?

JT Twenty-first-century transit plan, but this is the plan, right?

DG Well, in the 2020 document, when it first came out, it had no drawings. It's quite comprehensive, and it's the whole region, not just Chicago.

WW Presumably it's a commissioned research project or planning project.

DG I support this one because it's something Chicago needs so desperately.

JT Me too, but what was the program?

TW I support the fact that one is attempting to transform Chicago, but, gosh, I would have said that if you read the text and looked at the images, what is there to tell.

WW Let's keep it for the next round and then we can discuss it in more detail.

JT There have been better schemes than this that we didn't keep. I don't think this is anything. Are you going to keep it?

WW Yes, the other's sentiment is to keep it . . . On to the People Mover.

TW I really like it.

JT We have two jurors interested in the people mover, so we can leave that one.

WW OK, the next is the T 1 Tower in Paris, France.

DG I confess to being compelled by the top of that building. I would like to see this from more of a distance. It contains the mechanical, right? Is that what it is at the top? That's a bit unfortunate.

TW I do like to find out about this cable-truss thing.

WW That's where innovation can take place.

WS I would think the building would appear much stronger if it hadn't been deformed at the top like this, because there is no reason for this.

DG It is not apparent where the deforma-

tion has come from, it looks like somebody pinched it.

WW It'll give it a distinct appearance, a landmark quality. In the market, that's the only freedom left to the architect.

DG I like this one better than the one in the corner, which we kept.

JT I like this one too.

WW OK, the T1 Tower stays in. Next: Avery Fisher Hall—Lincoln Center, New York.

TW I was looking at it, I was trying to figure it out. What is this about?

WW It's about cellular structures forming a monolithic object, mysteriously lit at night.

JT I can give a discussion on this because I was involved in part of this. You may know the Beineke Library at Yale, where light comes from the inside through the stone. I am using a stone at Roden Crater which is even more transparent so that general light on the inside will come through the stone. This is to be done without the heavy structural expression that you see at Yale. The hall will be a stone building that glows from the inside. You can actually see the form of the theater on the inside, you can see 23 inches into the marble with a flashlight.

WW If it gets built, it's going to be pretty spectacular. I am not sure about the structure.

JT That was the proposal from about three weeks ago.

WW I think it could be fantastic if it could be built like that because it reveals its cellular nature and the form's codependence on the cellular nature for the enormous cantilever.

JT I have a great objection to how they use the computer to show light because everyone thinks that light is just put into a building and it can be made to look like that while it never looks like that.

TW I can't imagine that it will stay like

this because, frankly, the problem with Avery Fisher is the acoustics. It's very hard for me to get too excited about this proposal, not that I am against it.

DG Well, they would have to make a new hall.

TW Yes, I know but I would think that you would start with the acoustics, since that's the problem. I would be more interested in seeing how you support the stuff without the shadows.

WW Well, the auditorium is a box.

TW I guess it would be like glass as an exterior skin, then there would have been a full separation—a big separation.

WW I would vote for this scheme . . . And now for this: 505 Fifth Avenue, New York City.

TW I am not clear about what this is doing. The idea seems to be about playing with the building code, right? This is coming out and playing with a certain percentage of the building code. I wish that I knew more about how that actually could work.

WW There is a description here.

TW I thought I looked at the explanation, but I didn't see that the building was exploring the explanation, and I thought if, in fact, one could achieve that, then what are these spaces about? Why would one do that?

JT Yes, why?

TW One challenges the building code for a purpose. What bothers me here is that this doesn't. It seems like it's picturesque rather than to make a better space inside.

DG The whole project is purely about the zoning envelope.

WW It uses the regulations for the purposes of creating something picturesque, not picturesque in a negative sense, but something which is freer and seemingly looser than the irregularities of the buildings surrounding it.

TW I will look at it again.

JT Let's keep that in.

TW I like what you're saying, it's just that I don't see it . . .

WW On to the Washington Monument Visitor Center.

JT It's very "designy," but it's kind of interesting.

WW OK, I see heads nodding . . .

TW The fabric roof at Changi Airport Interchange is interesting because it's a retro-fit.

DG It's hard to say whether that's going to end up to be very elegant or not—the computer renderings are pretty awkward.

WS I like the idea.

TW I would have said the idea is better if one could have immediately resolved this relative to the existing structure. This structure exists, and this roof is new. The theme of penetration of light and structure are the two things I would be interested in.

WS This needs another detail. It just can't penetrate that light with a needle.

WW It's very painful. The overall form is enticing but not convincing. So Changi Airport Terminal 3 Airport Station isn't in?

JT No . . .

WW Greenwich Academy. There is interest in this, yes?

JT I like the landscaping.

TW It's a very interesting and tough idea. It is important to accept that underground systems are part of the landscape. I have heard a lot of good things about the Greenwich Academy.

DG Does the landscaping actually go over the roof as it's shown there?

TW Yes.

JT There were mullions which were interesting in the context of the Greenwich Academy and schools in general, in the sense that schools can be a lot more exciting than they have been. It's not

easy to do, it's a pleasure to do art, I will tell you that. You have to fight for your way . . .

DG How do we want to do this? Is this now to try to eliminate those that we don't think will be part of the final set?

WW Well, it can be that, or we can just vote and see and get a feel for it.

TW You had this idea that we had to have three votes for a scheme to make it through to the next round.

WW Yes, it just takes three, and you can make an argument for it. OK, University of California at Merced, Central Plant.

WS Yes, there is still something very interesting. Let's keep this. Let's vote.

JT So there are three votes?

WS Jordan House.

JT Yes, there are three there. You haven't voted for any of these.

WW I have not voted for anything yet, you are quite observant.

WS You don't have time.

WW Deerfield.

DG Yes.

TW You have three votes?

WW Yes. Elementary School: one, two, three votes

WW Then the Mega Tower.

DG Yes.

WS Yes.

JT There are five . . . Chicago Central Area Plan.

JT That's one we wanted to note and talk about.

DG Yes, I read through it. I guess I am the only Chicagoan here. We are looking at the Central Area Plan that SOM has been hired to work on, it isn't just illustrations. In that regard I think I was the only one supporting it. One would like more vision than is evident there.

WW I would vote for it if it really did propose significant changes for the city, but the scale of the interventions is very minor. A proposal of that size at the water's edge, in comparison to what the lakeshore as a whole means and what it deserves in terms of all the problems that it has at the moment, including all the problems it will have when this Central Area Plan is being implemented, is a complete misunderstanding of scale.

JT Again, to take the city on at this scale is almost akin to somehow making the coral aware that it's making the Great Barrier Reef. With zoning being what it is, I don't think the designers are able to do what they are thinking.

DG It's just plain not inventive enough. There are very good recommendations for this corridor, but if you don't know Chicago and know that corridor, then that is not acceptable.

WW The one thing that the plan seems to be doing is to define future development, that is, future building volumes as a way of densifying the center. From that point of view, it's not an area plan in the sense that one would know it to be comprehensive in terms of design, but it's essentially a plan for the development of certain properties.

JT This, again, is an important issue for us to discuss, and I don't think this is to be included as an example of that.

TW Yes, I think we need to discuss this further. I am sorry, are these the Chicago

plans for 2020? These are endorsed by the Chicago Plan, is that correct?

DG No. This is different than the Chicago 2020 Plan. It's the Central Area Plan only. The 2020 Plan is something much larger and more regional in scope, it deals a lot more with transportation.

TW For example, a statement like this: "create new grade-separated busways" is or is not part of it. I have no problem with that, but I then would have said one should then explore the various possibilities for that.

DG Again, you'd have to be more familiar with the local terrain to understand that this is all industrial use right now. That little green roadway here is all industrial now.

TW That's fine, but that makes the river premier public waterfront, it could mean making it green or putting hard-scape walkways on it. But I just say that you take that statement and show two possibilities or three or ten. There is zero wrong with the statement, I like the statement.

WW These are the key statements: "The vision, first of all, global Chicago. Make Chicago one of the world's great crossroads." I think it is anyway.

JT That's like telling your children to do something they are already doing.

WW Dulles People Mover.

JT I am interested in this one.

TW Yes, so am I.

JT Two anyway, but two won't keep it.

DG I think I would keep it. It's one of the few really tight schemes in the room. There's not much you can find at fault with it. I wish that I were just a little more excited by it.

TW I'd like to think that the structure that's the ceiling is a good structure.

WW What is your view on this structure, Werner?

WS My opinion is not yet formed. I have to go through it a little bit more in detail.

TW There's something tight and clean about it. When I think about some of the great infrastructures that existed in the country, I think about Dulles as a cool one; and the Washington Subway System is a good one; and I think this fits in with that rather well.

DG It seems like everything is covered, and it goes back to what the statement is clarity, lightness, I don't know about flexibility.

WW I would vote for this.

JT So how many votes are there? OK, so this is in for the moment anyway...

WW Avery Fisher Hall.

JT Let's just vote. I am for it.

DG I am for it.

WS Yes, maybe I am for it too, though I don't understand whether they are really able to realize the wall in the way that they are showing it.

WW Excellent, thank you, three votes... This next scheme here, Washington Monument Visitor Center.

DG No, no, I wasn't convinced beforehand.

JT I am interested in this.

TW Are there three votes? OK, there are.

JT It came down to nine?

WW From 24 schemes down to eight.

TW Does that alarm you?

WW No, I think it's perfect.

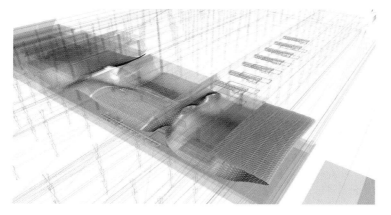

DG Can you read off the names?
WW Yes, they are: University of California at Merced, Central Plant; Jordan House; Deerfield SMT Center; Elementary School Number 11; China World Trade Center, The Mega Tower; Avery Fisher Hall; Washington Dulles Airport Automated People Mover Station; Washington Monument Visitor Center; Greenwich Academy.
TW I am not sure they should all be in.
WW We can reduce it further, if you want.
TW I feel that I'd like to discuss some that I think are underdeveloped, there is not enough information about the Avery Fisher project
JT I think that also applies to some of the projects.
TW I feel that there's totally speculative, and not developed, no solid substantive stuff here.
WW Right, for instance, when one compares the conceptual proposal for Avery Fisher Hall—with its lack of rigor but architectural promise—against Jordan House—which is well represented, but shows some fundamental problems in terms of the relationship between the planning of its interior and the free form—then there are two kinds of under-developed designs.
TW We know little about the interior, but we know the basic problem is an interior problem. Although I don't like the interior here, the way this might be experienced relative to the shape of the roof might make it quite interesting. For

example, I was just recently at the Piano project in Rome and the most interesting area was actually the area between the box and the shell. That was very power-ful. Yet when one was in the box of the concert hall, the experience was rather normative.
JT That's special regular architecture. There too when it meets, light comes off the stone. Actually it's where they meet. But this wasn't developed in the presen-tation. The idea is very nice—light comes through stone. This stone is remarkable, and it has less to do with the structuring of the building than in the Yale Beineke Library. In that way, it's quite interesting, but how do you show the interior struc-ture? It's the same idea for the Central Plant. I don't quite know how it works in the Central Plant, but they do have that perforated metal which could allow trans-parency. It depends on the lighting and how that really happens, I am not as sure of that.
DG Why can't we premiate something just on a simple idea? Why does it have to be developed all the way?
TW I know that stone this way can be very translucent. I also know that we can impregnate it with resin, creating large sheets that won't fall apart, that are virtually glass. But there is not one shred of evidence about the way this structure is supported and how the structure isn't the dominant element. If there was one thing that would let us know that the structure is not the dominant element, I might be more persuaded.

DG I still think though that the project needs more development.
JT It needs more development.
DG Sure, but if I am going to compare that to the plant, then I find it supremely uninteresting as a piece of architecture. The thing that interests me about Avery Fisher Hall is that it's a statement to begin with, and yet you are absolutely right in everything you say, there's no development. At a certain point one would expect more material develop-ment, but just for its pure conceptual value, this scheme is much more inter-esting to me to think about as an urban

gesture, to think about many other issues regardless of the detailing than the Central Plant.

WW The point is that you are comparing the Hall with the Plant, and I don't think you can compare them.

JT What you see there is what you are going to get.

WW That's correct, but the Hall is more ambitious, it takes more risks and ultimately it could be an utter failure as a building.

DG This is SOM—it won't be a failure.

WW I am just saying that it takes risks.

TW I don't see that there is enough risk. Everyone knows that the problem with Avery Fisher Hall is the acoustics of the main volume. There's no explanation of how one attends to its central problem.

WW We are all able to bring certain critical criteria to the readings of these schemes. Tod's criticism is ultimately the most important. The problematic part of this project is that it's completely under-cooked, and this is maybe something that which we can see in some of the work here: there's a tendency towards surface research and towards formal research rather than towards research in terms of program.

JT What you are also saying about these new skins is that there are skins that are laminated as you laminate glass. Stone and glass get laminated so that you can have, for instance, stone on the inside and glass on the outside, which is better for cleaning as stone often gets quite dirty from pollutants.

TW You can also add UV layers and all sorts of stuff. Let's see, maybe we should keep all nine of them. Maybe we could criticize some of them more. I don't see any reason that we need to be unanimous on all of these, except Wilfried hates the Jordan House, and we each don't like some of them, but there's a lot of unanimity among the others.

JT I actually like the Jordan House elevation. All of the great graphics are terrific. I am quite interested in the drawing on top, and then I like this tiny elevation at the very bottom which shows the way it meets the site. But you are right, Wilfried, in your criticism.

WW I don't have any objections to what Tod is suggesting. But on Jordan House, let's just cast our minds back to people like Paul Nelson or Frederick Kiesler. People who really developed the idea of free-form and made it a consistent spatial and formal experience. This was what in the fifties and earlier architects like Josef Frank were after. Jordan House seems to me to be just an external form superimposed on a centralized Palladian plan.

DG It is a Palladian plan, isn't it?

WW I have recently looked at many of these blob designs for another jury. I was frustrated by the lack of a relationship between the form of freedom that is sought by, and given by computer technology, and the space conception as well as its material construction. That's the worst thing about these blobs. These things are basically inconsistent.

TW This is not a very free plan, or free form, it's an extremely determined form.

DG It's an industrial design form.

JT It's like your DVD player.

TW Yes, that's why somebody called it bombastic. It's hardly free form.

WW How much money will go into the making of the curvature, as opposed to the occupation of the interior?

WS Yes.

JT That's why I vote for this little project, the café, and this one here in the corner. After constructing a place myself, I know that these building systems have been involved in the predetermination of the architectural design, not to mention the fact that we used foam core to model the design. If you have a curve in one direction, that's a big expense right there. It's a hugely expensive wall, but then if you have a compound curve which is ellipsoidal or something like this, boy, there goes the building expense, and we are going to somehow, somewhere chase this with some new system. Maybe we are going to have bubble systems blown up and maybe we shoot against that and we pull them off, but there will be these new things that the contractors and the system makers will follow with their developments, but they will only follow if we make designs like this.

DG But those techniques, and those technologies, are more and more available. One thing I am disappointed in today is that I don't get excited relative to technology in this room. There are all sorts of ways to do curves. I would want to see how the house is going to play itself out. I know it can be done. It's not the most economic building system out there, but still even compared to five years ago, it's more possible, more available and accessible to architects. There are precious few examples in the room that . . .

JT . . . push that.

DG Yes. From a company, or set of companies, that have probably more access to technology than most of us—computer technology—that's a little disappointing to me. I see more innovation in the graphics and the renderings, I see it a lot less in how the buildings are put together. I don't know, Werner, if you feel the same way in terms of technological innovation.

WS This is my impression. It's a little sad because the firm was very famous in the fifties, sixties, seventies, and even at the beginning of the eighties for the perfect weaving together of advanced architecture and advanced technology in all fields. This is really falling apart here. I would like to support Wilfried with his criticism on this bubble type, there's nothing negative about the bubble shape of the building itself. This would be such a great chance to develop even a new technology to construct such a roof, it's not that expensive and it's not that difficult. We've done several of those very

irregular shapes. You can pay for that—this is not the point—but what comes out of it for me is, if I am doing some completely other shape for a building like this, you typically ask how it's organized on the inside? What is the technological background? Is there a new way of interpreting this house? Which means, is there another type of washbasin another bathtub, doors have handles, or is everything voice controlled? When I am look closely at this, it's an absolutely conventional house with a new shape. One might say: OK, so it's a little bit fashionable to put such a shape on top of it.

TW It does have sectional possibilities. The direction of the conversation seems to suggest that SOM is not doing very adventuresome work. But it's also trying to work on smaller scale projects, which I don't think it had pursued before. Whether it's the house or the carpet tiles . . . in a certain way they are sacrificing some of the penetrating research of the fifties and sixties that also had an aesthetic. Today SOM is questioning the edges of the architectural world. Our architectural world is coming from people like James Turrell, who are adding a new dimension that wasn't present in the fifties and sixties. It seems to fly in the face of many of the technological things that were developed.

JT It's true, there are several issues, and certainly architecture as design, or

as fashion, is one of them. We do see certain things entering with fashion, and there are other things that are driven by function. We were talking before about what is being driven by things like ADA and building codes. There are a lot of things that have to change, that you have to push out and building codes and ADA are driving a lot of things right now. More than we want to even admit. There are places where they are pushing these things. Some places, not too many you know, when you go to build a skyscraper. This is not an experimental project, these things are going to have to work. This is a company that does that.

TW We all so fully endorsed the Mega Tower. I wonder whether we ask if that is really pushing the envelope in a way.

JT It isn't always pushing the envelope that does it though.

TW Or what's the envelope that's being pushed.

WW It's the envelope as structure, as dilating structure, which is the strongest part about it.

DG There's something about this one, it seems to be the least forced project in the room. Like the Dulles project, there's no mess in it, it's what it is; it's clear. I feel the same way about this high rise, and I love this—I don't know if its bamboo or more of a cigarette idea—this kind of a double wall, where they are not doing the same thing. It's more than a functional double wall, there's some kind of aesthetic payoff, and I can't tell, it seems like its also a structural move.

JT Yes it is.

TW Initially, it seemed that there was a very strong conceptual idea about the structure, and then on further inspection it appears more conventional, the diagonal bracing is only giving it the lateral bracing it would not otherwise have.

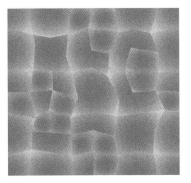

This then means it's been relegated to a secondary position.

WS Yes, the bamboo idea is a little bit misleading because in the end it does not act like bamboo. The bamboo is anchoring this perfect cube, this perfect pie, which is then stabilized against buckling by those built-in diaphragms. But this is neither a perfect pie, because it's diagonalized and you have to look out of the building and it doesn't have those diaphragms that the bamboo does. But forget about this bamboo sketch, I think this building is, for me personally, convincing because of its clarity and its simplicity and there is nothing to be discussed, because there's nothing overdone or underdone, it's just what it needs.

JT I like the ghosting in the two different scenes, its almost like a double figure.

TW Yes, it really is working, and its also part of the aesthetic, and I find that really good.

WW It's one of the strongest projects here.

JT But it also is really what SOM is about; you take that one and that one; and this one in Paris, and I think those are the real classical aspects what this firm is about.

WW The Mega Tower has certain Chinese qualities about it, which relate it to the pagoda composition.

JT And strangely, it relates more to this picture here than to these antennas. That's the antenna, and they have all of the forms that come out of a stupa. First of all there is a sphere, and then the cube, and then there is the antenna on the top.

DG I wish there was an image of the interior of this atrium. I don't know if we all realize this, but this great hollow space two-thirds of the way up in the building is pretty amazing.

TW I very much like this. I would say that this represents the traditional SOM posi-

tion, and the Greenwich Academy, which I am excited about, to me represents the new SOM. What impressed but concerned me about SOM was that it was a very big firm. We see here that there's a sense that the firm is interested in work as well on a more intimate and personal scale.

DG There's another reason to recommend this project. It points to some of the good news in the room, which is that there's a different kind of interest in the environment that isn't just functional, it is not just the data on the wall.

JT The Greenwich Academy was very well worked out with the green thing you are talking about, with the siting and all that sort of thing.

DG Yes, it works functionally, but there's an aesthetic sensibility that shows it as one of the more contemporary projects in the room. The way building and landscape become intimately integrated for aesthetic reasons, that's why I keep going back to Deerfield. It's not as strong a scheme as this, but it's trying to do something that I think is wholly contemporary, in the sense of a weave of landscaping ideas, sometimes literally, sometimes not, with ideas of building so that they get wrapped up and confused with one another. The Greenwich Academy is very clear, very elegant, more so than the Deerfield project, but they're relatives of one another.

TW I like this construction system—the use of wood . . . I think it's going to be very beautiful.

DG It's great to see it getting built, too.

WW I am quite satisfied by this selection because it represents a cross section of interests. Craftsmanship and design are demonstrated by such schemes as the People Mover and the Central Plant. There are some areas of innovation and of risk taking. To find nine out of a field of 62 is not so bad.

DG We have not talked about the Washington Monument, I didn't vote for that one, I'd enjoy hearing more.

JT Neither did I.

DG What you can say about Avery Fisher Hall in terms of development, you can say about this one too.

TW Very close to it. While it's a valid criticism, I wish we knew more about how one would manipulate the landscaping to find space beneath the monument.

WW There's a section right at the top.

DG It feels like a sketch problem.

JT On the second one down you can see the tilting of the site. The idea you would come from a long way away in order to enter it rather than everyone gathering at the base of it to go up, I think is very nice.

DG So you would come under one of these disks, and you come up the side of it.

JT You can see the disks at the second one down.

WW It could be sublime. The question is what the difference in light intensities will be between the illuminated monument and the ring.

JT Well, the presentation of this scheme and that of Jordan House, and this presentation here are good. This one here was convincing in presentation, while we actually didn't see that much behind it. Those are the four that would get my graphics vote. I find it very interesting that everyone is going to a dark background with the illuminated schemes; it's very much like classical painting.

TW It's a valid criticism. Its weakness is that we don't have a plan. With a plan, we might know more about one would manipulate the landscape to find space beneath the monument. It represents a sort of state of SOM and maybe all of us right now. There are so many possibilities. One is looking for a direction the firm is heading. And at the moment, it's like akin to a teenager—a person very much in search.

WW Are you all then as well satisfied as I am with these nine? Or would you want to make a final cut?

DG I would vote that we keep the nine. One reason for keeping the nine is because a lot of them aren't developed enough to be put on more of a pedestal. The variety is there. If we were to reduce it to four or five, we would have to have more information. If we were to try and reduce it, you could start by comparing the schools. We haven't talked much about the Elementary School, but we were agreed that it's not necessarily a new idea. It's just really well done, and it's a school one would like to be in. But

if one were choosing schools, I might be a lot more interested in this for the effects it would produce inside the classrooms.

TW This has a clear concept—a very clear conceptual model. The building, of course, has lost something in that translation but may have gained something. It's very ordinary, buildable work.

WW The scheme's quality lies in the fact that it's not dependent on its elevation, which is quite plain, but on its relation to the context.

WS I am still struggling with some issues. The question I am asking myself is why SOM is doing this jury exercise. Is it because they want to have an internal ranking? I don't think so. I think they are doing it because they want to have some advice, some ideas, some criticism. This criticism is independent from the fact whether we pick one, or ten, or twelve. We now have nine and this is OK. The significance of going through this jury for the last hours is that there are many designs which are not homogeneous. You could think that they came out of different practices, from different continents, that the architects were of different ages, had a different education, and so on. On the one hand, this might be very liberal or democratic phenomenon. But on the other hand, I think it would be great if a practice like SOM had a common basis that you could identify in looking at their buildings. This must not mean that the Chicago office should be doing the same designs as

the New York one. Try looking at sheet number eight of the Chicago Central Area Plan, there's somebody developing a future scheme and giving you a practical idea of how the future will appear. Look at this pond with the frogs jumping. This can't be the future. This is a sketch of the forties or fifties. This is trying to establish a bit of coziness. And then and there's the real opposite when we are look at the Beijing World Trade Center Tower. This is developed from its technology, its environmental considerations, its façade technology, and things like that. Here's something that is tending towards the future. This is a real piece of development within the thinking of SOM, taking the basis of the Hancock, and all those other buildings with which SOM got famous, and developing them further, involving green technologies, energy-saving principles, and so on. This is therefore why we did not find the presentation of the Chicago Plan acceptable. It's simply a mess to look at those six or seven sheets.

TW. I agree that is something to look for and also to try to find a series of principles that would guide the design of that firm. Another tendency may have to do with so much opportunity for the individual to speak. I see buildings that seem to be designed by several people. It is almost as if someone might get a fixation on a mullion detail, as it would be, or some aspect of a building, but not the whole building. We have certainly seen that in the athletic complex (Tianjin

Stadium) where we see that it's made of a series of separate buildings. But we also see it even within a building where it seems designed very, very clearly by several different people with different aesthetics and intentions.

DG I am interested in this question of whether the work is too pluralistic or not, or whether SOM as an entity, or set of entities, should or would want to be more defined in terms of identifiable buildings. The reason I was arguing for some of the research was that this is the intellectual push that is all too rare. One wants to support it because it helps the practice to stake out the territory in more than one sense. Whether it leads to identifiable SOM buildings or not, I'm not so sure. I would be a little afraid of the branding that could come with this.

WS I want to add one sentence, because I want to avoid any misunderstanding. My personal goal would never be a recommendation that these 1,500 architects, or however many there are, draw in the same style, I am not interested in one product after the other leaving the factory. But it would be awfully important that there's a basic, common understanding of where the practice is going, how it uses materials, how it implements the structure, how environmental issues are addressed, and things like this. The arrival at a basic understanding—in German we say *Haltung*—the definition of an attitude or attitudinal approach should be really important.

TW This attitude, this approach should occur in the research so that . . .

DG . . . so that the research is carried through . . .

TW . . . and that then would enable you to continue to operate pluralistically.

WW If there's something that distinguishes large practices from smaller ones, then it's a large practice with a certain authority. The jury noticed last year that if anybody can do something,

if anybody can push research, then it's the large practice with the authority of decades of knowledge, decades of practical experience, and senior designers behind it. In this context, partners would turn to clients, saying to them, yes, let's spend a couple of weeks thinking about this brief, and then we'll come back to you, and we'll put forward a number of options. And we'll put forward a number of concerns that we have, so that this freedom that experience and authority bring, authority through knowledge, might best serve architecture and built environments as a whole. We see that this can lead to schemes such as the Mega Tower or even to things that we didn't select, forms of research, such as the early ideas for the carpets. It's an interesting field that just hasn't gone far enough. Milliken must be paying SOM quite a few bucks to carry though that kind of research, and it's exactly that domain of research that needs to be pushed in order to improve design quality everywhere. All these concerns and frustrations that we've put on the table today, coupled with the recognition, are important signals to everybody working at SOM, that every office, whether small or large, has to deal with these long-term concerns. These are long-term concerns about the profession of architecture; about its contribution to society. But more specifically, the concerns that Werner mentioned with regard to how cohesive, how comprehensive a practice's approach ought to be, need to be answered before a practice's design quality can be raised at all. It's important to review the practice's ethos of the fifties, sixties, and seventies, and even of the early eighties.

WS Yes, or even to reestablish them.

DG The projects that we have selected today have one thing in common: for the most part the thinking is clear from start to finish. SOM Chicago is intending to set

up a "think tank" on technology, which other small and large firms are also doing. An architectural practice's ability to labor over creative work and also still stay up with the production schedules is a hard thing to balance, and maybe that is where a larger firm has more wherewith-all to be able to extend its activities into areas of research.

JT Do schools have that possibility?

DG It depends if the schools are funded well. What's great about the schools is that they can think in a less unfettered way. We can pick and choose what we want to deal with in a school.

JT Do different companies that make these systems give you products and samples?

DG Some do, others like a Boeing, which has just come to Chicago, would prefer to be partners with a company the size of SOM.

WW At a school, you don't have to go right to the top. You can start at the very bottom for instance, in the case of a piece of furniture. If a student is interested in some kind of reconstituted paper, he or she will go to the internet, do some research and probably get some free samples from a manufacturer, who is generally happy to see it used in a design. From the individual initiative of a student right to the individual initiative of a teacher, you will be given support at whatever level because the enthusiasm of the individual is infectious. Ultimately there's growth and recognition by a wider circle of industry. There might

be further funding of research, maybe at $10,000, maybe at $100,000, and so on. That's how these things develop. There are schools of architecture that don't do research because the definition of research in architecture is a very muddy one. In the scientific area of architecture, in other words in building technology, it's more easily defined. That unfortunately is a misconception, the pursuit of architecture as a whole is fundamentally a piece of research. It's a question of how you define parameters, concepts, and how you define the continuous development of concepts into a material reality. It's not so much someone having a brilliant idea. Many architects spend a whole lifetime thinking about certain problems.

TW We might suggest that next year, for each of the projects presented, each submitted scheme should have a clearer point of view relative to the research. We have even endorsed some that are mostly refined presentation. We have to ask what is the value of this for SOM? On the other hand, some other goal is necessary. What are the essential issues that the firm should pursue? That's the issue of integrity.

WS Yes, it's necessary to say that we cannot celebrate the best here, because we do not have enough information about the single entries. We only can get a feeling for the tendencies. There's a total lack of description of how the structure works. There's a total lack of description of what materials are used.

DG We should note that most of the work up here is in some form of a preliminary design. We are not looking, for the most part, at built structures.

WS Yes, but what I am saying, following the first idea for a building, which might be about the shape, as soon as I put color to a drawing, I think about material and light.

JT Absolutely.

WS I have to answer the question whether this is a titanium-glass powder-blasted surface, what happens to it when the sun is setting, or what it is that I am describing. You can't find it. In the case of Jordan House the text says something about a wooden type of structure, which is very easy to be erected. This is completely boring because wooden frames were done 100 years ago. It would be different if this were a wooden grid shell, which Frei Otto did 30 years ago and which enables you to do any shape especially with irregular curves.

JT That's something else.

WS This is what's missing for me: a small step towards a certain direction.

WW One of the reasons why you don't get that is because the computer is brilliant in formulating almost finished representations. That's the big misleading power of the computer.

JT Forty years ago we would not have had this information. Look at Le Corbusier: he would do this little sketch and that's what he's going to make. They may not have even modeled it, they might just go to drawings, and even

working drawings of 40 years ago. People would say, "you can't build this, you can't build this from these, there's not enough information here."

DG Yes, I look at a lot of work on the walls that are just in form of sketches. The representations on the wall, while they look finished, I don't ever take to be finished. There's a lot of schematic work on the wall. I went around the room today evaluating these things in terms of ideas, comprehensive or cohesive or not, evidence of some kind of vision, evidence of some kind of search, or research, one or both. I kept coming back to Jordan House, because it's the loudest on the wall. But orange as it is, it's not an idea about materials yet, I don't even want to know whether it's made of wood. As a sketch, it's more about the CD player as an industrial design form, it's a lot less interesting to talk about it in material terms. How was it last year?

WW There was a similar discussion on these issues and on graphics.

DG I expected to come here and see things that were at more advanced stages of . . .

JT . . . development. It would be a good thing for all of the teams to come in here and to look at the work the way we've looked at them, to see the schemes together, to see how they stand up in terms of their graphics. I agree with you that there needs to be diversity within a firm. You would hope for that and for some singular voices to come out. At the same time, you expect a certain level of thought and presentation, which is not there.

DG It's all over the map.

JT Yes, the criticism that was here last year is still evident. We need to have a better description of the charge they were given, and what they are doing; if it's renovation, if it's redevelopment, and so on.

TW So, there must be better descriptions?

WW It was clearly put to them even for this occasion and for the first occasion, that there should be a descriptive text, no longer than 400 words, describing the main intention of the scheme. There's no excuse. Architects are notoriously bad at writing. They loathe writing, they are absolutely afraid of writing, and even if you say 400 words to them, which is not a lot, they put off writing to the last minute. When they then start to write, it turns out to be an essay of epic proportions, which they find very difficult reducing. As you can see from some of these texts, because they are far longer than 400 words, you know it's a problem. How do you edit the textual information? How do you edit the visual material into something cogent and concise? This is a perennial problem that we have at universities, in offices, and so on. Those schemes that have coherent presentations, it's clear that somebody has obviously thought about these sheets, being next to each other, following in logical sequence, they must have spent two weeks or so on the content and layout.

TW How do we represent the work? When we think about presenting something to colleagues in a closed environment, as opposed to presenting, let's say, a client: who should be addressed? It must be the client and the issues that relate to the project.

JT We were always most embarrassed by the way we presented to each other.

TW Still it's important for colleagues to come and look at the work.

WW These are constructive recommendations, which will be passed on to SOM as a whole. It's been a long day and a critical review of SOM's work. We've reached consensus on these nine schemes, I am grateful for that. In closing, in my capacity as the editor and on behalf of SOM, I would like to thank you all for your involvement, your time, and your frank participation. You've been a tough and constructive jury.

Jury Biographies

Douglas Garofalo

Douglas Garofalo, AIA, has established an internationally renowned practice in Chicago that produces architectural work through buildings, projects, research, and teaching. The work of Garofalo Architects has been widely recognized, through commissions, awards, publications, and exhibitions for innovative and creative approaches to the art of building. With projects that vary in scale and location, Garofalo has actively pursued architectural design to include forms of collaboration that cross both geographic boundaries and professional disciplines, extending conventional design practice by taking full advantage of the capacity of electronic media.

Garofalo is a professor at the University of Illinois Chicago School of Architecture and a facilitator at the design lab Archeworks. Garofalo graduated from Yale University in 1987 and was awarded the prestigious Skidmore Owings & Merrill Foundation Traveling Fellowship. He graduated from the University of Notre Dame in 1981.

James Turrell

James Turrell was born in Los Angeles in 1943. His undergraduate studies at Pomona College focused on psychology and mathematics; only later, in graduate school, did he pursue art. He received an MFA in art from the Claremont Graduate School in Claremont, California. Turrell's work involves explorations in light and space that speak to viewers without words, impacting the eye, body, and mind with the force of a spiritual awakening. "I want to create an atmosphere that can be consciously plumbed with seeing," says the artist, "like the wordless thought that comes from looking in a fire." Informed by his studies in perceptual psychology and optical illusions, Turrell's work allows us to see ourselves "seeing." Whether harnessing the light at sunset or transforming the glow of a television set into a fluctuating portal, Turrell's art places viewers in a realm of pure experience. Situated near the Grand Canyon and Arizona's Painted Desert is Roden Crater, an extinct volcano which the artist has been transforming into a celestial observatory for the past thirty years.

The recipient of several prestigious awards such as Guggenheim and MacArthur Fellowships lives in Arizona.

Tod Williams

Tod Williams has been principal of his own firm for the last 30 years. The partnership of Tod Williams Billie Tsien and Associates was formed in 1986. The studio of 15 people is well known for its wide range of projects, its exceptionally high standards, and work which emphasizes the importance of place and explores the nature of materials.

Built works include Feinberg Hall at Princeton University, Hereford College at the University of Virginia, Phoenix Art Museum Addition and Renovation, the Neurosciences Institute in LaJolla, Natatorium at the Cranbrook Schools in Michigan, Mattin Student Arts Center at Johns Hopkins University, and The American Folk Art Museum in New York City.

Williams has been a teacher for over 30 years. In 2002 he held the Eliel Saarinen Chair at the University of Michigan; he presently holds the Louis I. Kahn Chair at the Yale.

Werner Sobek

Werner Sobek was educated as an architect and structural engineer at the University of Stuttgart, Germany, where he also obtained his PhD in structural engineering in 1987. Having worked for Skidmore, Owings & Merrill in Chicago, and for Schlaich, Bergermann & Partner in Stuttgart, he was appointed full-time professor at the University of Hanover, Germany, in 1991. One year later he founded his own engineering consultancy, Werner Sobek Ingenieure, which has since grown to an office with 70 employees in Stuttgart and 15 in Frankfurt, Germany.

In 1995 Werner Sobek was appointed successor of architect Frei Otto and took over the famous Institute for Lightweight Structures at the University of Stuttgart. In 2001 Werner Sobek was also appointed successor of structural engineer Jörg Schlaich. The new institute that emerged out of a fusion of the two chairs headed by Werner Sobek focuses on research on new materials and new concepts for lightweight structures, such as adaptive building envelopes.

Wilfried Wang

Wilfried Wang is holder of the O'Neil Ford Centennial Chair in Architecture at the University of Texas at Austin, where he teaches design and architectural criticism. Together with Barbara Hoidn, he is in partnership in Hoidn Wang Partner, Berlin. He received his BSc and MSc degrees in architecture at the Bartlett School, University College London, and is a registered architect in England and Germany. He has taught at the Polytechnic of North London, the Bartlett School, Harvard University, the ETH in Zurich, the Städelschule in Frankfurt, and the University of Pamplona.

From 1995 to 2000 he was the director of the German Architecture Museum in Frankfurt. He has curated exhibitions on 20th-century architecture in Austria, Ireland, Portugal, Switzerland, Finland, Sweden, Greece, Spain, and Germany, as well as monographic exhibitions on the work of Alvaro Siza, Boris Podrecca, Herzog & de Meuron, Hermann Czech, Diener & Diener, Eileen Gray, Sigurd Lewerentz, Mart Stam, and Heinz Bienefeld. Thematic exhibitions include *The Ecological Challenge to Architecture* and *Power and Monument in German Architecture.* Symposia include "The Ecological Challenge to Architecture" (with catalogue) and "Umbau—Conversion" (with catalogue). Wang is the author of various publications and essays on aspects of 20th-century architecture.

Automated People Mover Station
Washington Dulles International Airport

Chantilly, Virginia
Designed 2001–02

As the first airport designed for commercial jets, Eero Saarinen's design for Washington Dulles International Airport revolutionized the airport experience. Saarinen created a compact Main Terminal serviced by a system of mobile lounges that formed a seamless link to a series of concourses in the midfield. The design for a new Automated People Mover Station at the Main Terminal of the airport is one element in a comprehensive plan to replace the operation of the mobile lounge system that was first introduced by Saarinen in 1962.

The new Automated People Mover Station is bounded by the existing Main Terminal to the north and the control tower to the south. The primary space of the station is a trench excavated between these existing elements and is clearly defined by two four-foot-thick cast-in-place concrete walls. These primary concrete walls define the major processing areas in the station—the security mezzanines and train platforms— to create one continuous space which is 1,000 feet long and 105 feet wide. The floor in this space is a simple terrazzo plane that floats between the two primary concrete walls to the north and south. The floor folds in one move from the security mezzanine down to the platform, guiding people as they circulate between levels. Two glass pedestrian bridges traverse the width of the station, directing arriving passengers to enter an illuminated glass escalator tube which serves as a transition between the new station and Saarinen's original baggage claim area.

Circulation to and from the primary space of the station occurs in smaller antechambers which are accessed through apertures in the four-foot-thick concrete walls. In contrast to the smooth, monolithic qualities of the primary spaces, the walls of the antechambers are richly textured with three-dimensional faceted pre-cast concrete panels. The circulation elements of the station, including the 400-foot-long train tubes and elevator enclosures share a common language of faceted translucent glass forms which are illuminated from within. Brightly colored train and elevator cars move as shadows behind the patterned glass, subtly announcing their arrival to passengers in the station.

The faceted forms of the pre-cast walls and glass circulation elements are echoed in the design for the concrete roof structure of the main station space which spans 105 feet from north to south. The concrete roof structure resolves issues presented by the long span in combination with heavy live loads from the mobile lounges driving above, while creating a unified pattern of structure, luminous membrane, and skylights. A consistent rhythm along the length of the station is maintained in the ceiling design despite the complexity of the conditions occurring on the driving surface above and in the station below.

Skylights allow the maximum amount of natural light into the space and provide views to the sky, the control tower, and plinth wall as it rises towards the terminal. Above ground, the skylights are as flat as technically possible, respecting the simplicity of the terminal's south elevation as they quietly reveal the presence of a subterranean station below.

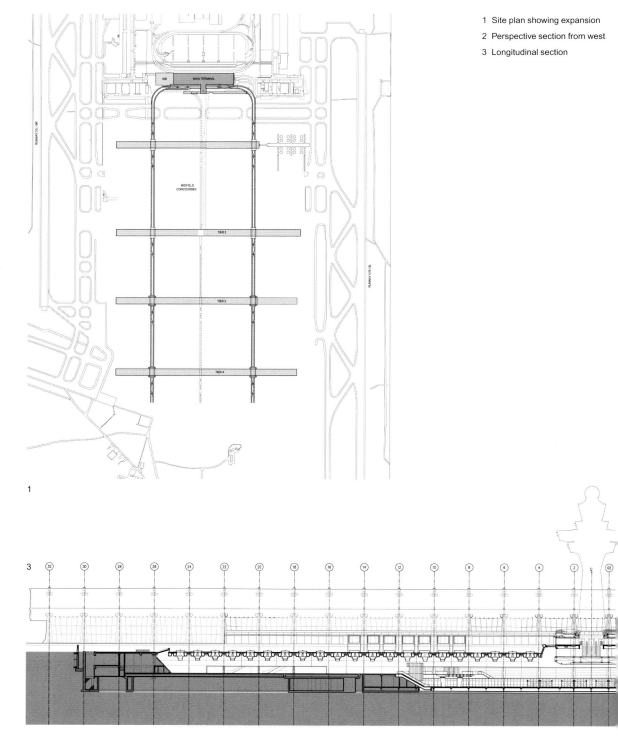

1 Site plan showing expansion

2 Perspective section from west

3 Longitudinal section

1

3

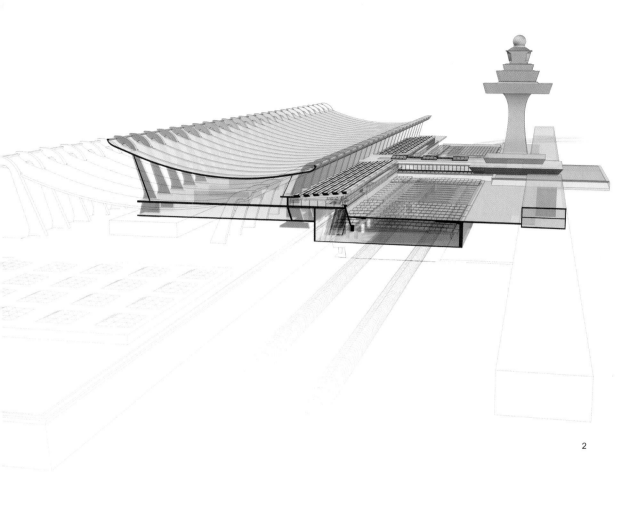

2

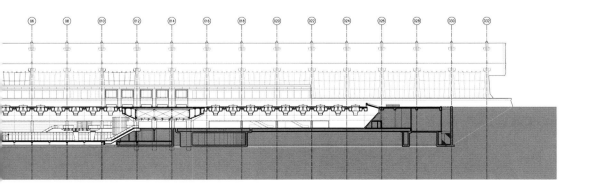

4 Design component diagram

5 Departure-level plan (elevation 305 feet)

6 Security mezzanine-level plan (elevation 270 feet)

7 Platform-level plan (elevation 255 feet)

8 View of security mezzanine

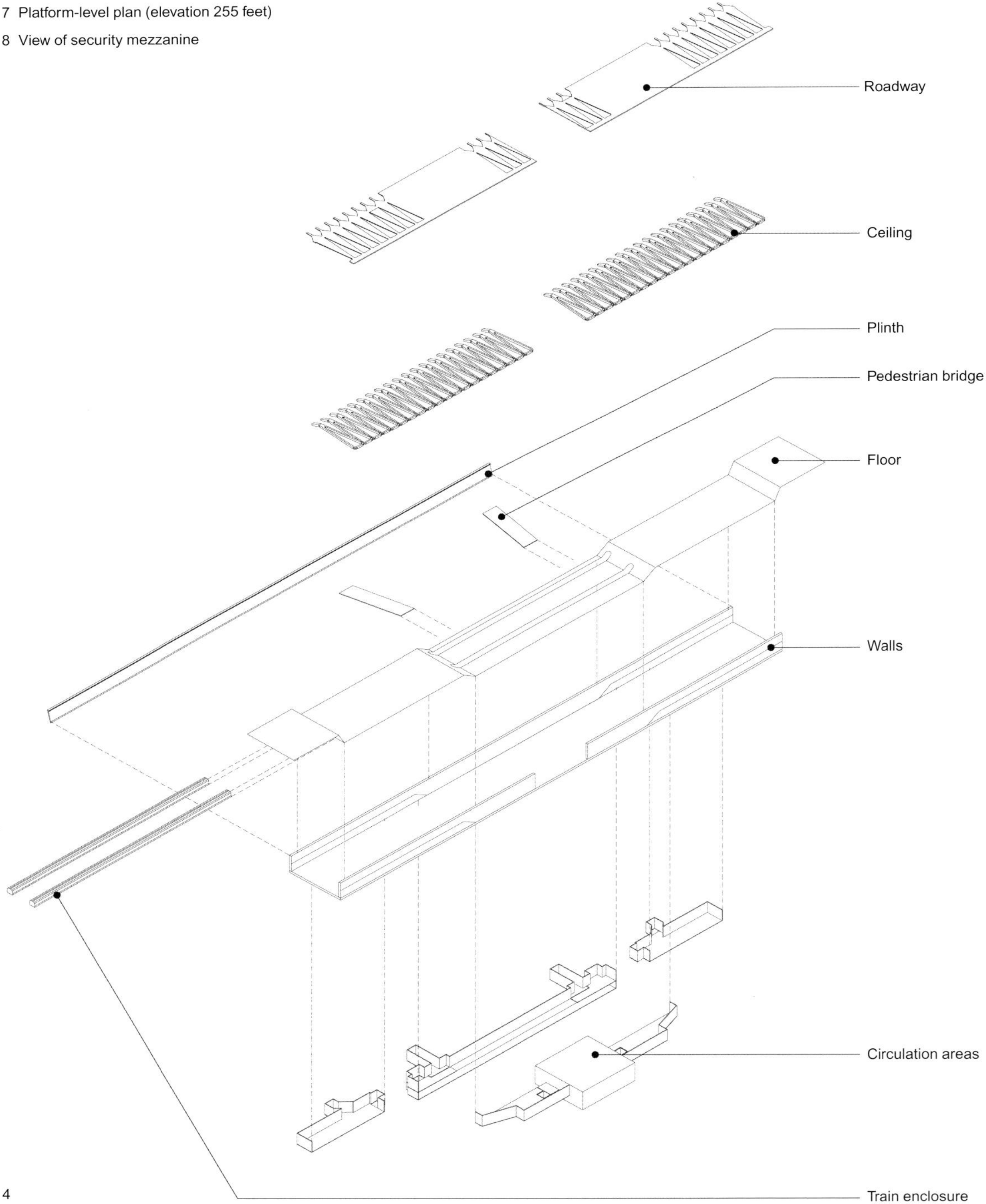
Roadway
Ceiling
Plinth
Pedestrian bridge
Floor
Walls
Circulation areas
Train enclosure

4

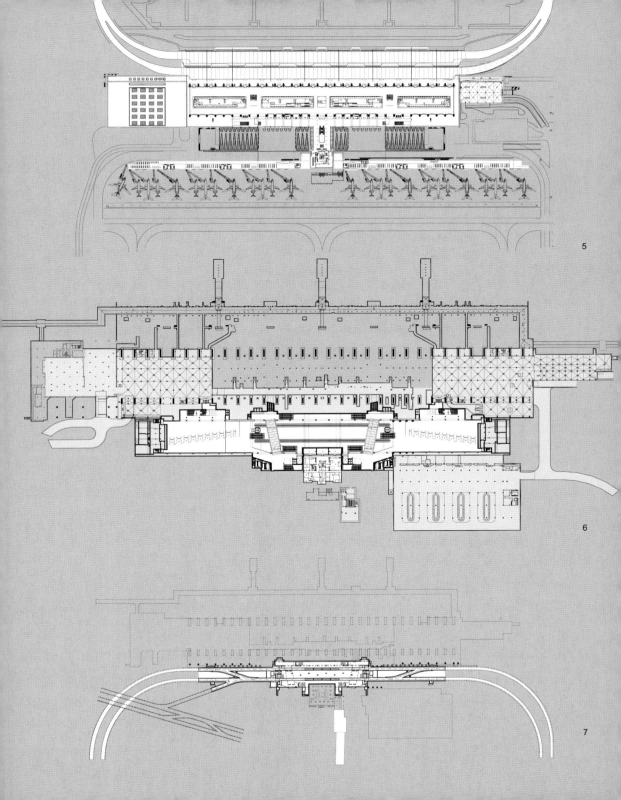

5

6

7

9

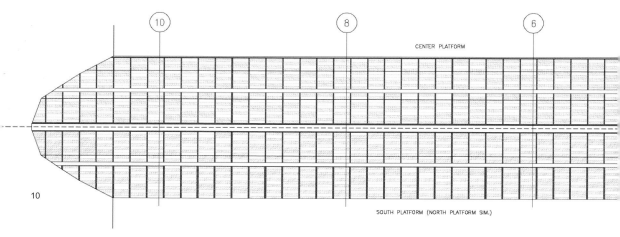

10

CENTER PLATFORM

SOUTH PLATFORM (NORTH PLATFORM SIM.)

9   View at platform level

10 Unfolded train enclosure

11 Glass pedestrian bridge

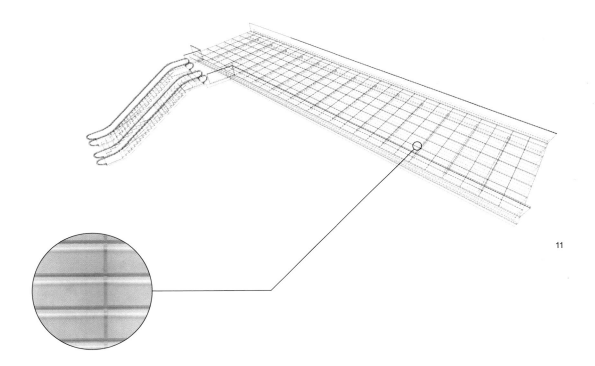

11

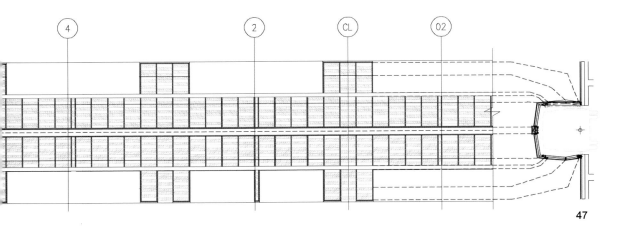

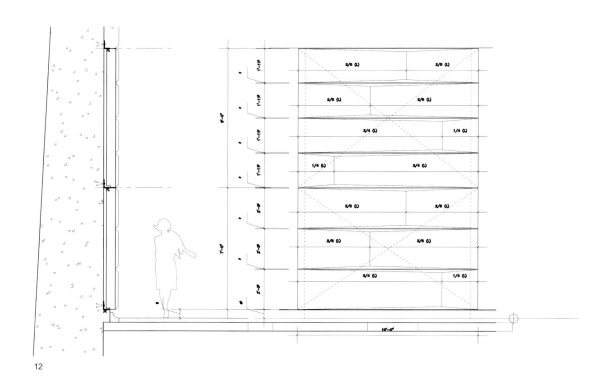

12

13

12 Detail of faceted concrete wall

13 View of concrete wall

14 View from mobile lounge holdrooms

15 Transverse section

14

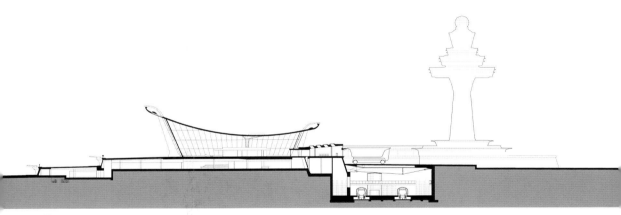

15

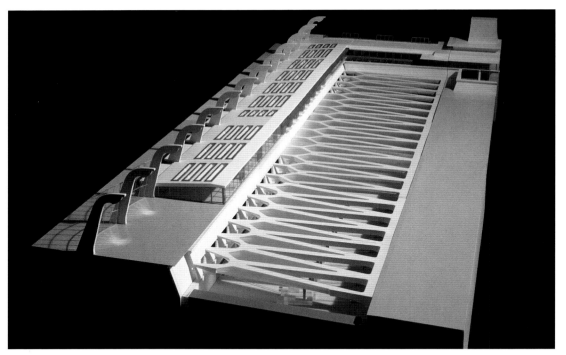

16

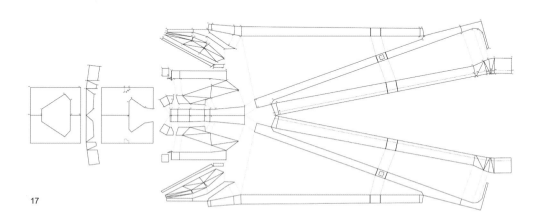

17

16 View of roof structure

17 Unfolded steel formwork

18 Roof-structure geometry

19 Sections through roof structure

20 View of center platform

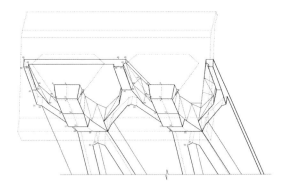

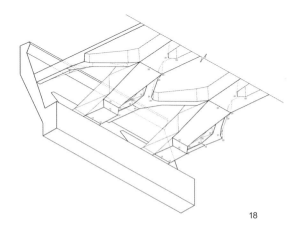

18

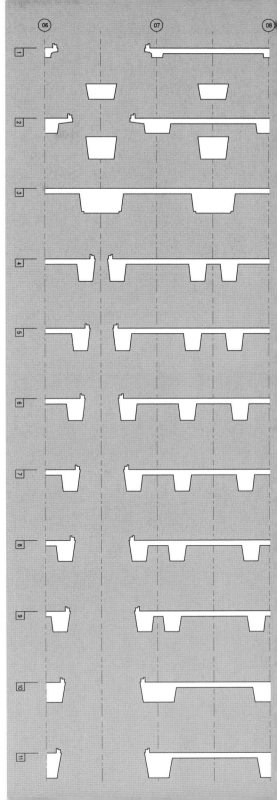

19

Central Plant Building
University of California at Merced

Merced, California
Designed 2001–02

UC Merced is a new Campus in the University of California system to be located in California's rural Central Valley. The first phase master plan proposes a library building, a classroom building, and a laboratory building that come together to form a quadrangle around the Campus Green. The Central Plant will service these buildings and provide for future growth of the campus.

Situated on a small bluff above an irrigation canal, the site offers flat, green fields with mountains beyond. As the campus grows around it, the context will become one of a university campus ordered around an urban grid where the plant will be situated near a street intersection.

The plant has three main components that play a key role in achieving the high sustainability goals of the new campus, targeting 20 percent lower consumption than any existing UC campus. The plant building is a 41,000-square-foot building that contains electrical equipment, pumps, chillers, boilers, and cooling towers stacked on three levels. Adjacent to the plant building is a Thermal Energy Storage (TES) tank 61 feet in diameter that rises 75 feet above the street intersection and holds 30,000 ton-hours of chilled water for the campus's needs. The third element is a one-level telecommunication hub. The plant and tank sit on top of a concrete plinth that is partially embedded in the ground. The plinth and the telecommunication hub help enclose the service yard. These central systems connect to the other campus buildings via a utility tunnel.

The TES tank, which will be the tallest structure of this phase of the campus, is wrapped in an outer layer of metal panel system. The diamond-shaped panels are two feet wide, four feet tall, and are shingled to corrugated and perforated metal panels. Each layer performs a specific and discreet role. The rigid cement-panel backing offers acoustic protection and provides support for the rain screen membrane, which keeps water out. The metal panels protect the layers under it from damage. This separation of roles allows all the metal panels to be perforated. The independence of function allows the external layer to float free of the underlying surface, visually lightening the surface. The layered assembly, behind the metal panels, changes in response to program and acoustical needs, thereby creating variations in the way light interacts with the perforated wrapper. This exploration of transparency and lightness using perforated metal is an extension of a previous SOM project, AboveNet LA, which wrapped a secure computer facility with a perforated metal "veil." Unlike AboveNet's veil, which provided sun protection, the Central Plant's perforated metal layer is part of the wall system and plays a more integrated role.

A thin band of channel glass wraps the base of the building. This element not only allows visibility inside and provides acoustical protection, but also provides enough natural light during the day to reduce electric energy. As the ribbon of channel glass is mounted just above the floor surface, the floor works as a "light shelf" to bounce diffused light up into the upper reaches of the chiller and boiler rooms, enhancing the daytime lighting efficiency.

Inspired by the Visible Human Project, which makes the human systems transparent to students of medicine, the central plant attempts to make mechanical-electrical-plumbing systems as well as building systems transparent and understandable to students of engineering.

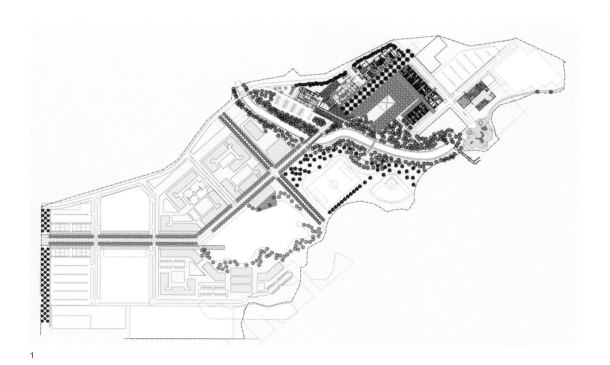

1

2

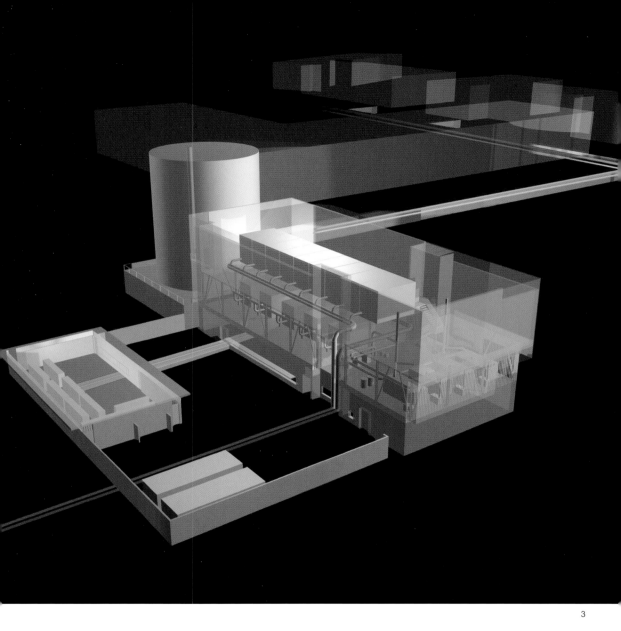

3

1 Site plan

2 Site model

3 Program diagram

4

4 View from south

5 Channel glass wall cladding

6 Ground-level plan

7 East-west and north-south sections

5

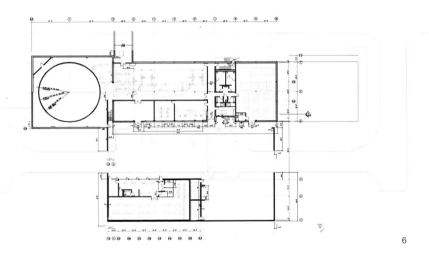

6

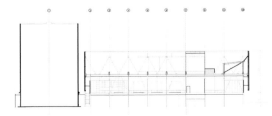

7

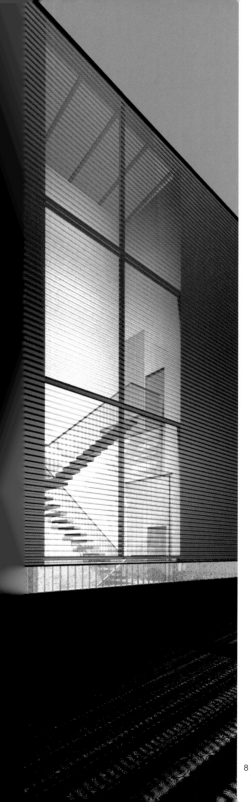

8   9

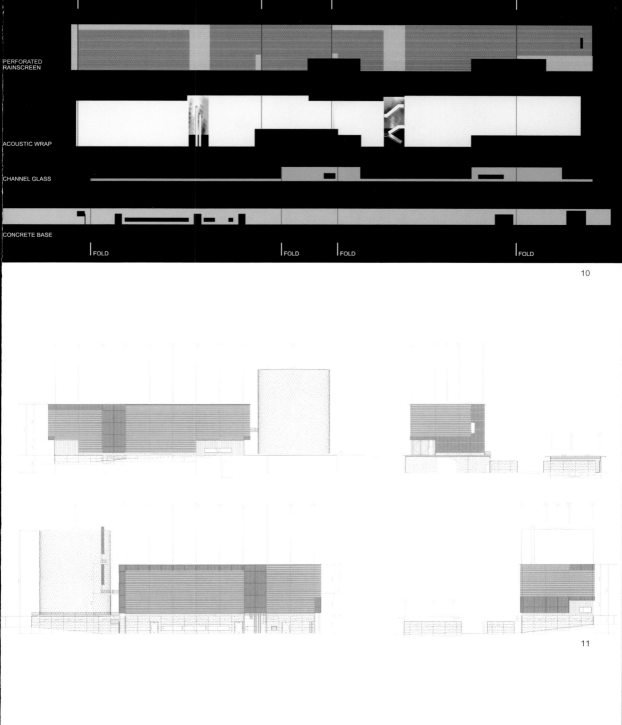

PERFORATED
RAINSCREEN

ACOUSTIC WRAP

CHANNEL GLASS

CONCRETE BASE

FOLD   FOLD FOLD   FOLD

10

11

61

Concert Hall Lincoln Center

New York City
Competition 2002

The concert hall typology has traditionally been a reconciliation of the specific volumetric requirements of the interior performance room with the architectural language and contextual issues of the exterior building envelope. The design of a new concert hall for Lincoln Center seeks to blur the distinction between the interior performance and the exterior expression. Glass and translucent stone panels permit a kind of X-ray of the structure and infrastructure of the inner hall, giving visual access to the backstage spaces which are usually concealed or suppressed. The translucency of the façade gives a veiled visual access to these spaces, conveying more completely the process of a production and its performance.

The 2,300-seat performance room is enveloped in a three-dimensional network of concrete vierendeel-type trusses and fin walls that form the structural support for the open void at the building's center. The structural network also serves as a multi-level circulation gallery around the performance room, and the open areas between the truss chords serve as support and breakout spaces for the hall. In the backstage areas, the open areas in the trusswork define a series of practice, scenery, and green rooms that are at times visible through the building's translucent façade, depending upon relative interior and exterior light levels. This thickened layer of support functions within the space of the vierendeel network mediates between the interior spaces and the exterior façade, changing on the outside as the performance progresses inside.

Access to the building via two entrances at street level and two entrances at plaza level creates a porous base that animates the corner of 65th Street and Broadway. The simple prismatic building form addresses the Neoclassical composition of the Metropolitan Opera House and the New York State Theater on the plaza side, but creates an equally emphatic address on 65th Street, where a garden, café, and breakout area occupies the space beneath the cantilevering hall. There are secondary access points from the sidewalk level at Columbus Avenue and the reflecting pool level of the Vivian Beaumont Theater, designed by SOM's Gordon Bunshaft and completed in 1965. The resulting multi-directional access mitigates the urbanistic shortcomings of the complex's elevated plaza. The hall may be entered from each of the four sides and links these entrances to a main stair and series of escalators which bring visitors to a large reception room overlooking the plaza.

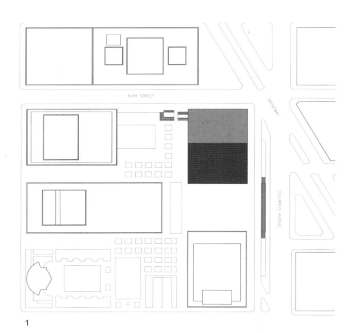

1

2

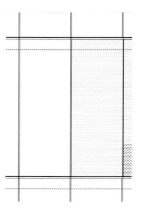

3

4

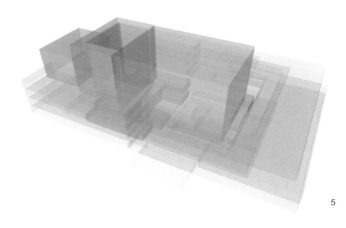

5

1 Site plan

2 Translucent stone

3 Exterior wall section

4 Structural concept model

5 Main program volumes

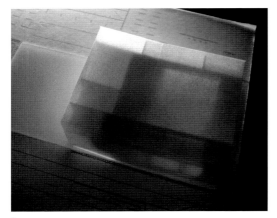

6

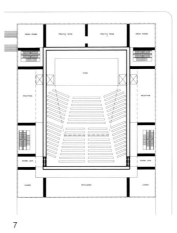

7

8

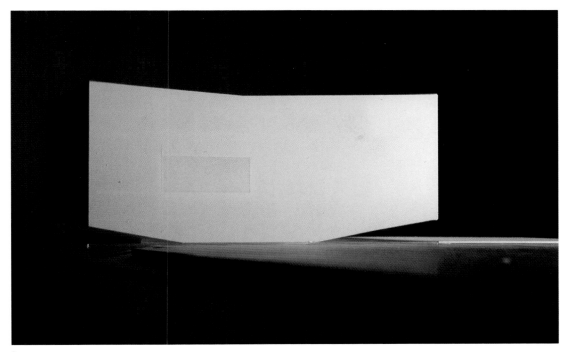

9

10

11

11 Plaza view

12 East elevation

13 North-south section

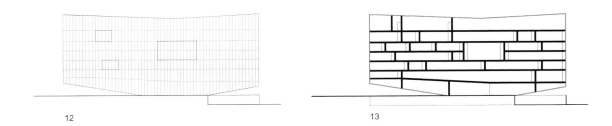

12

13

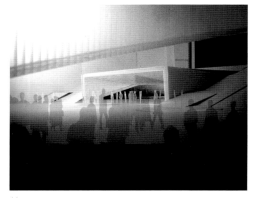

14

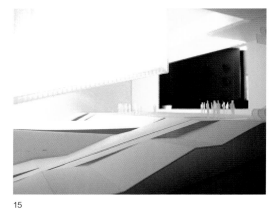

15

16

17

18

19

View from Columbus Avenue

Science, Math, and Technology Center Deerfield Academy

Deerfield, Massachusetts
Designed 2001–02

The Science, Math, and Technology Center (SMT) is the latest addition on the Deerfield campus, overlooking the beautiful landscape of the Deerfield Valley. The project will complete the campus structure, following the edge of the plateau and framing the Big Lawn. The structure is clinging to the landscape, weaving its way through it just as the Deerfield and Connecticut River had done thousands of years ago. By extending the architecture into the landscape, the two become unified; building walls become retaining walls. The program spaces are filled in between the walls, stepping down towards their ends, extending the natural topography with garden roof terraces on different levels.

One arrives at the main entry of the SMT by following the wall that reaches out to the historic center of the school. The entry opens up to a three-story-high atrium and to the view to beyond. This central gathering space brings all the sciences together: astronomy, biology, chemistry, computer science, environmental science, and physics. Adjacent to the atrium are special activities displayed in rooms behind switchable LCD glass. The 80,000-square-foot building houses classrooms, laboratories, and office spaces for math and the sciences, as well as a number of special program elements. The auditorium, planetarium, and entries deform the parallel straight walls. Through this deformation, the curved walls map the dynamics of the program.

The programmatic nature of the project generated the thought of creating a team including visionary minds from several fields of science and art to outline tangible design ideas. A forum was organized, bringing together internationally-known artists, scientists, historians, and architects to implement ideas for the project.

One concept resulting from these dialogues employs an 18-inch opening at the roof of the building. Direct sunlight will enter through that aperture above the atrium and project a light spot on the opposite wall. Throughout the day, the projected light will wander along the brick surface, becoming a bright white light at noon when the incoming ray is unbroken by the prismatic glass of the skylight. Throughout the year at noon, the white light will trace a figure eight, the *analemma,* visualizing our calendar and the elliptic path of the earth around the sun. It will open the minds of the students and connect the building to the universe.

The intent of the building is to illustrate humankind's impact on the universe, as well as its place within it. The building creates a partnership with the earth by building into it and placing the removed soil on its roof, by conserving and returning storm water to nature, and by its energy efficiency and regulations for good air quality. Mechanical systems, lighting, and structure are fully integrated in the primary walls, which provide flexibility for the partitions and allow for uninterrupted floor and ceiling planes.

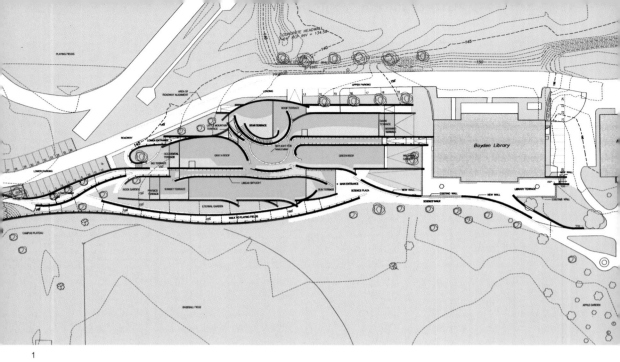

1

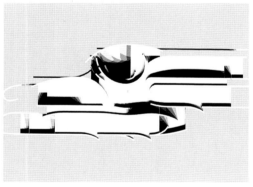

2

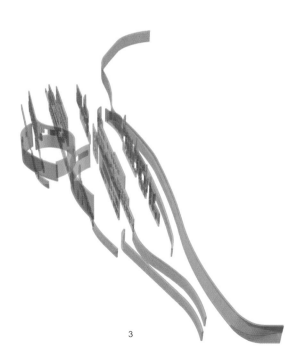

3

1 Site plan

2 Roof shadow study

3 Brick walls

4 Model view from west

5 Geometry studies

6 Model view from south

7 Model view from southeast

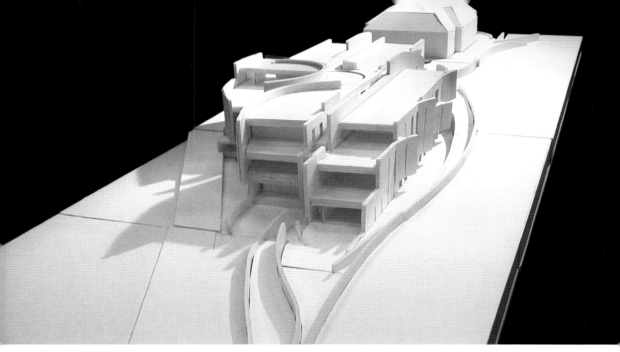

4

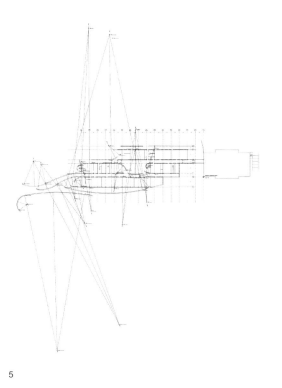

5

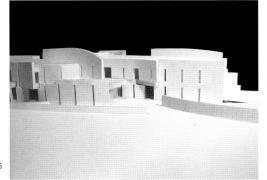

6

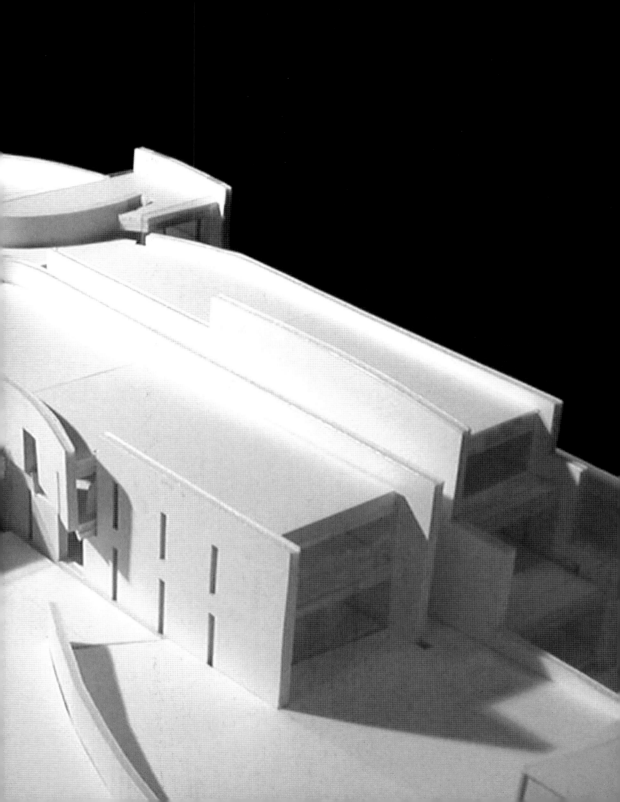

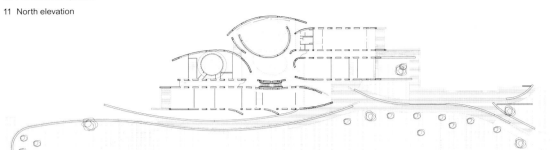

8

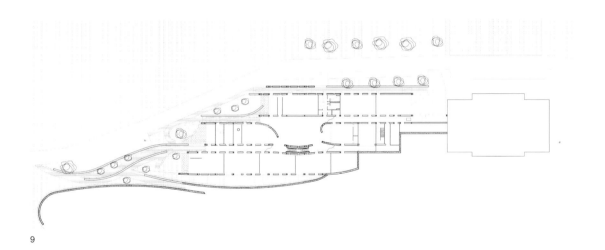

9

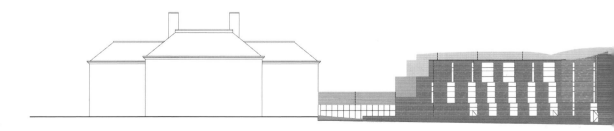

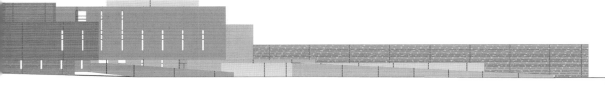

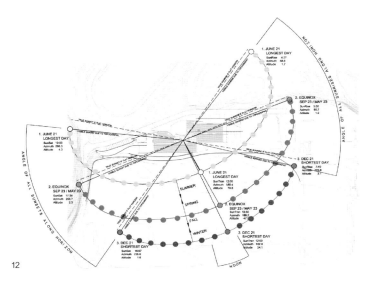

12

13

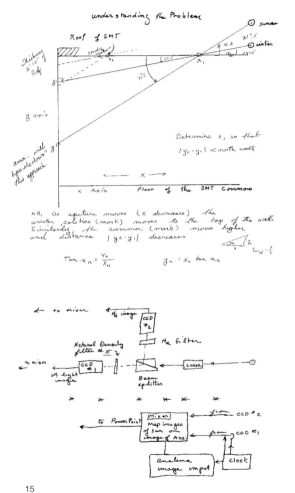

understanding the Problem

Roof of SMT

Thickness of Roof

y axis

Ana. will lips sidedown the approach.

sunan

71°.5

α3

winter

α_4) 24°.5

24°.5

71°.5

x_2

x_1

Determine x, so that

$|y_2 - y_1| <$ north wall

x : Axis   Floor of the SMT Commons

NB. As aperture moves (x decreases) the winter solstice (mark) moves to the top of the wall. Similarly, the summer (mark) moves higher and distance $|y_2 - y_1|$ decreases

$\tan \theta = \frac{y}{x}$

$\tan \alpha_n = \frac{y_n}{x_n}$ $y_n = x_n \tan \alpha_n$

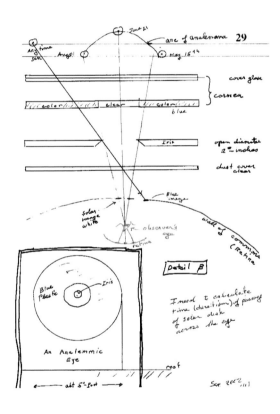

June 21

Any time
SMT

Angle!

arc of analemma 29

May 16th

cover glass

cornea
color   clear   color
blue

Iris

open diameter
2½ inches

dust cover
clear

Blue
image

solar
image
white

wall of commons
(Retina

observer's
eye

retina

Detail B

Blue
Plastic   Iris

An Analemmic
Eye

roof

about 5½ feet

I need to calculate time (duration) of passage of solar disk across the eye

Scr XXX²
111

to mixer   Hα image

CCD
#2

Natural Density
filter #5½

Hα filter

to mixer
CCD
#1

wt light
image

Lense

Beam
splitter

*   *   *   *   *

to PowerPoint

Mixer
Map images
of sun on
image of Ana

from CCD #2

from CCD #1

analema
image input

clock

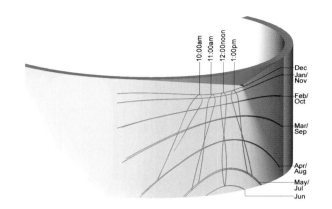

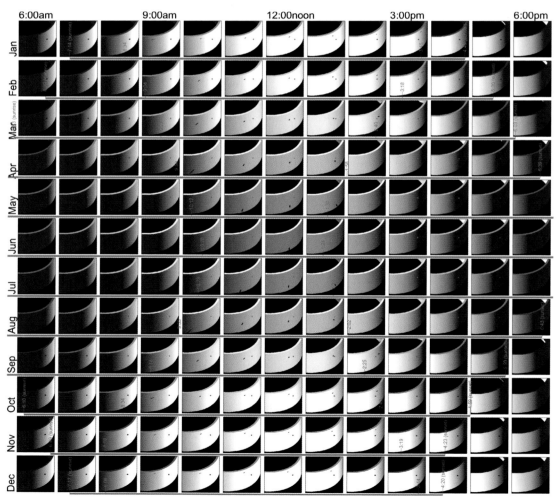

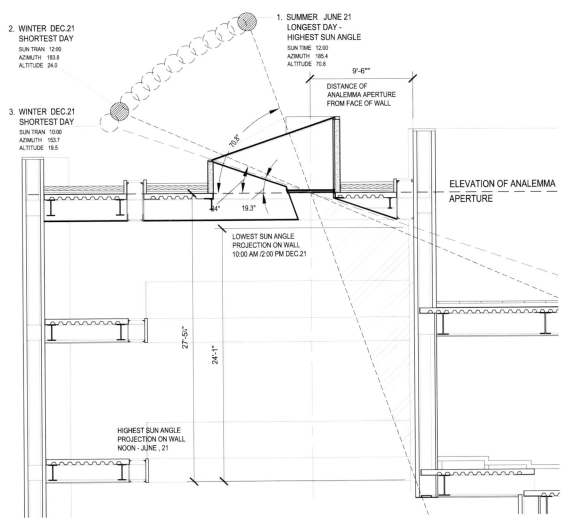

2. WINTER DEC.21
SHORTEST DAY
SUN TRAN 12:00
AZIMUTH 183.8
ALTITUDE 24.0

1. SUMMER JUNE 21
LONGEST DAY -
HIGHEST SUN ANGLE
SUN TIME 12:00
AZIMUTH 185.4
ALTITUDE 70.8

9'-6""

DISTANCE OF
ANALEMMA APERTURE
FROM FACE OF WALL

3. WINTER DEC.21
SHORTEST DAY
SUN TRAN 10:00
AZIMUTH 153.7
ALTITUDE 19.5

70.8°

24°   19.3°

ELEVATION OF ANALEMMA
APERTURE

LOWEST SUN ANGLE
PROJECTION ON WALL
10:00 AM /2:00 PM DEC.21

27'-5¼"

24'-1"

HIGHEST SUN ANGLE
PROJECTION ON WALL
NOON - JUNE , 21

18

Elementary School Building

Fairfield, Connecticut
Designed 2001–02

The design of an elementary school for five hundred students on a heavily wooded site in rural Connecticut provides an opportunity to integrate nature with the day-to-day experiences of the students. The prevailing elementary school plan typology—a series of double-loaded corridors with special functional elements at either end—is reconfigured to allow existing trees to perforate the plan, creating a series of courtyards that become outdoor classrooms within the building volume. This introduction of natural light and air permits a compactness to the plan that minimizes disturbance of the site and prevents the unnecessary removal of additional trees.

The plan is organized by grade level, kindergarten through fifth grades lining the east and west edges, with shared elements—art, cafeteria, gymnasium, music, resource and gifted rooms, special science—in between. At the center of the plan is the library/media center, which opens onto an outdoor courtyard. Access to the building is accommodated through two primary entrances: a bus drop-off on the building's south side and a parent drop-off on the north. This separation of entrance routes avoids the necessity for a perimeter road encircling the school, which results in each classroom looking onto a wooded area, as opposed to a parking lot. The bus drop-off area also serves as the playground, minimizing the amount of paved area and storm-water runoff. Grading of the site is designed to balance the amount of "cutting" and "filling" of existing topography, avoiding the need to import or export material from the existing site.

The north and south building façades are composed of single-wythe insulated concrete masonry units and structural steel window frames that permit a variety of openings without requiring additional structural framing. Heat gain from southern exposure and heat loss on the building's north façade are mitigated by the relative opacity and high R-value of these façades. The east and west-facing façades employ full-height glazing with a low-emissivity coating to permit maximum daylight penetration to the classroom spaces and improved views from the classrooms to the adjacent wooded areas.

The courtyards are arranged according to existing tree locations, and each has doors that allow access from instruction and circulation spaces. The forms of the courtyards create a reversal of the figure-ground reading of the plan, whereby the sunlit volumes of nature become figures within the larger building volume. Circulation occupies the residual spaces between the courtyards, creating a continuous space onto which all classrooms and instructional spaces open. The courtyard walls are comprised of insulated glass panels measuring 4'-0" by 11'-6" and 4'-0" by 9'-6" in an aluminum mullion system. The top of each curving courtyard is defined by a continuous 27-inch-deep curved steel beam that supports the roof decking above and anchors the top edge of the glass wall below.

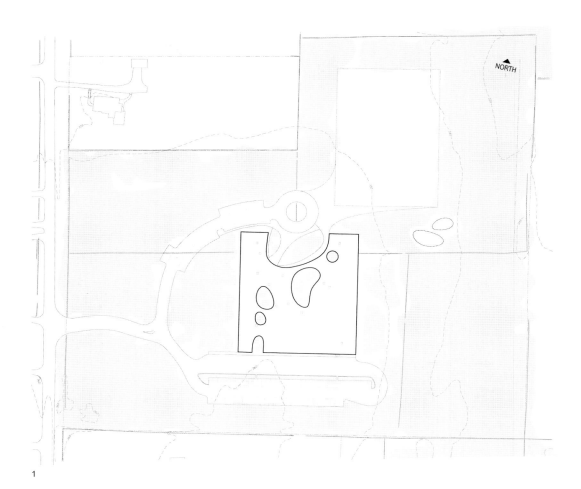

1

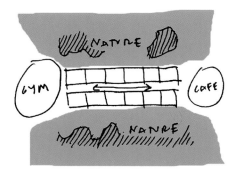

2

1 Site plan

2 Plan concept diagrams

3 Site model showing wooded context

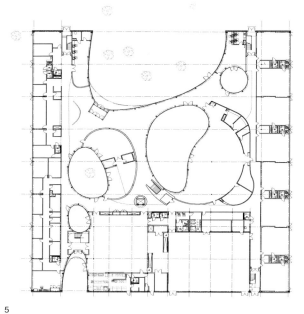

5

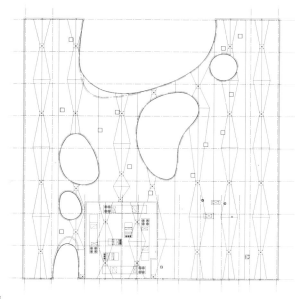

6

7

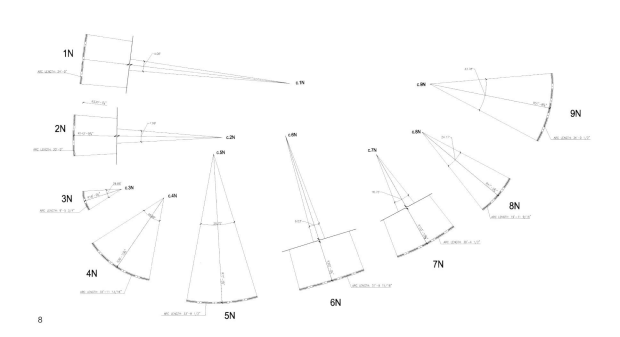

8

9 Ground-floor slab plan showing control joint pattern

10 Framing model

11 Model photograph showing skylight locations

12 Model photograph showing gymnasium and cafeteria

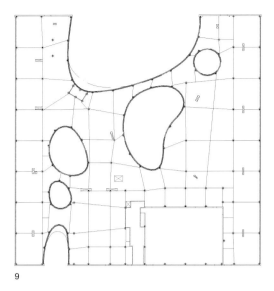

9

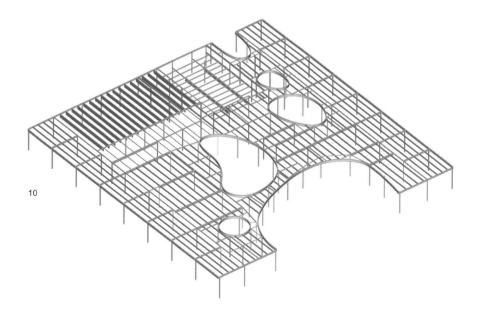

10

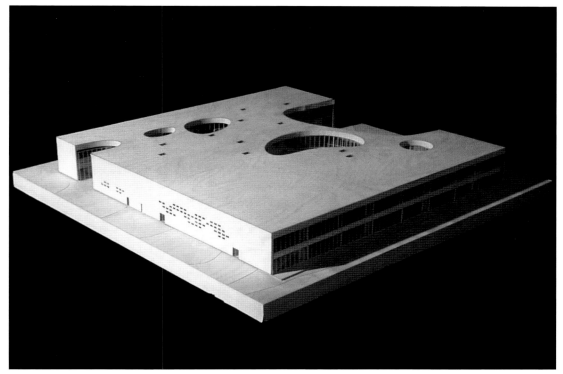

11

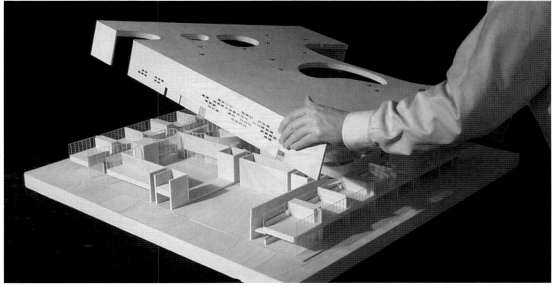

12

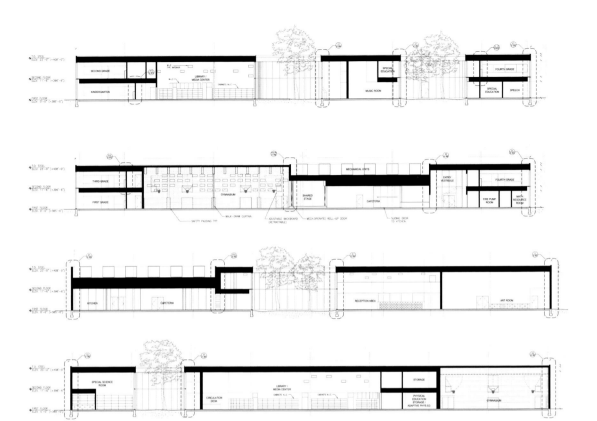

13

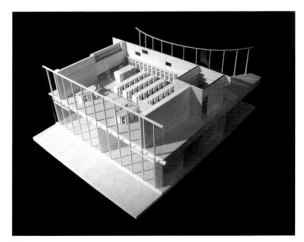

14

13 Building sections

14 Classroom model

15 Model showing curtainwall at courtyard

16 Single wythe wall with structural window frames

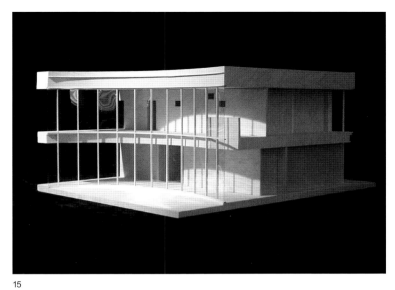

15

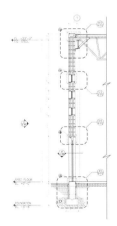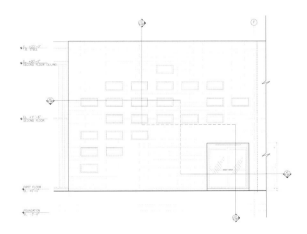

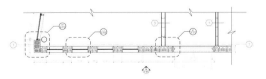

16

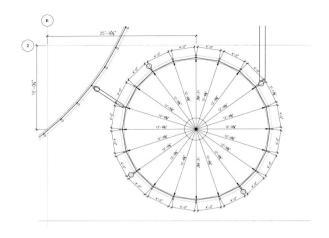

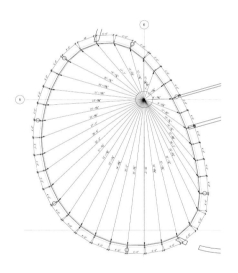

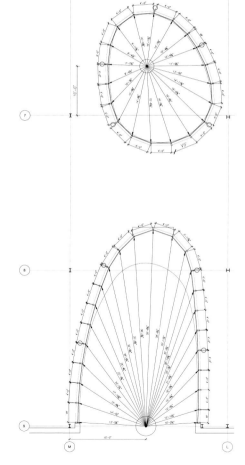

18

19

20

Academic Building Greenwich Academy

Greenwich, Connecticut
Completed 2002

The new incarnation of Greenwich Academy brings the daily academic experience tangent to the natural beauty existent in the campus. The uninterrupted landscape carpet of the upper campus is extended to create a new edge, as the topographical level of the pond and fields slip beneath.

Academic life exists between these two landscapes, the upper and lower. In the process of fitting together the four academic clusters between the strata—Science and Math, the Humanities, the Arts, and the Library—important adjacencies emerge, points of contact where exchange can occur between the discrete areas of learning. Recognizing that times and academic needs change, the boundary of any given discipline is pliable, comprised of a perimeter of flexible partitions which over time can expand and contract in response to the needs of the academy. Casework, furniture, and equipment will be on wheels, mobile and unconstrained.

In a process of architectural and intellectual archeology, a series of light boxes pass vertically through the horizontal academic strata, revealing the function at each in a "moment of clarity" that appears as an array of light, transparent objects interspered among objects between the buildings of the existing campus. These objects accept daylight to the center of each cluster and are evidence of the academic life beneath. The Academy, committed to the inclusion of Nature and Light in the formation of a learning environment, wished to extend this interactive dialogue into the domain of the perceptual experience, "creating a sense of wonder." Artist James Turrell was invited to collaborate and explore his ideas of light and environment in the Upper School classrooms, light chambers, and the surrounding campus.

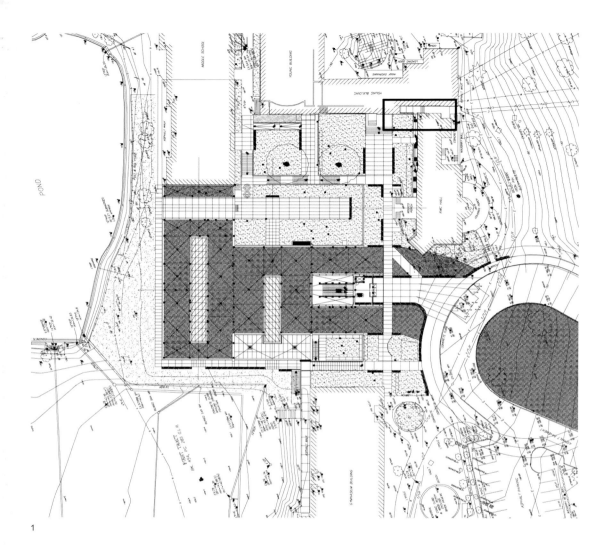

1

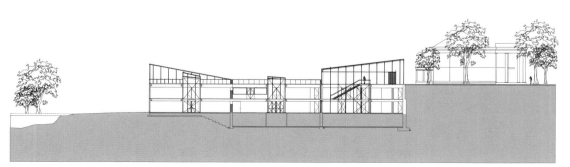

2

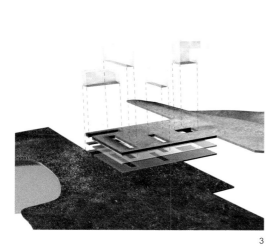

3

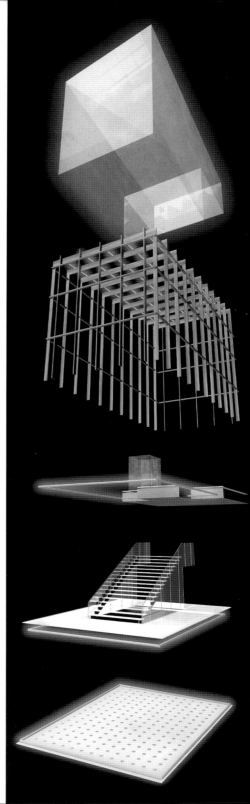

4

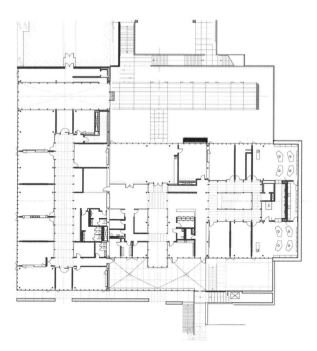

6

7

6 Second level (terrace)

7 First level (field)

8 Elevations

9 Model view from east

10

11

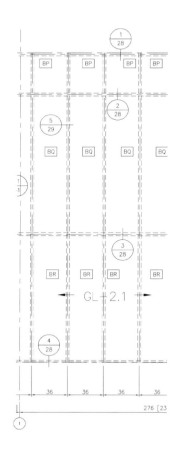

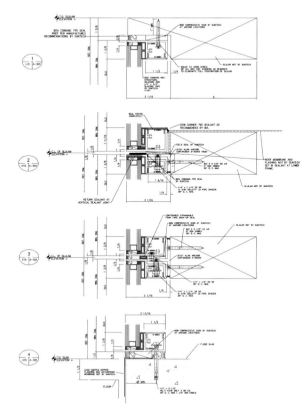

12

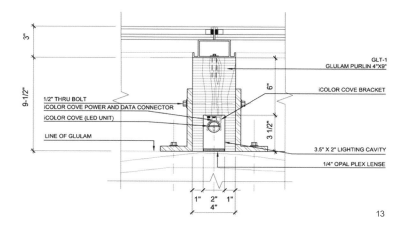

3"

9-1/2"

GLT-1
GLULAM PURLIN 4"X9"

iCOLOR COVE BRACKET

1/2" THRU BOLT
iCOLOR COVE POWER AND DATA CONNECTOR

iCOLOR COVE (LED UNIT)

LINE OF GLULAM

6"

3 1/2"

3.5" X 2" LIGHTING CAVITY

1/4" OPAL PLEX LENSE

1" 2" 1"
4"

13

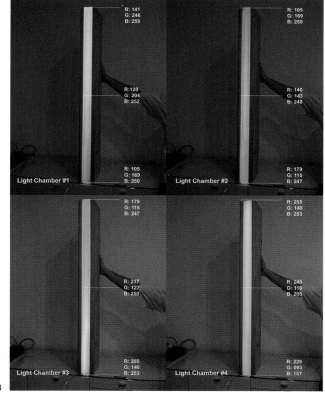

R: 141
G: 246
B: 255

R: 105
G: 169
B: 250

R:120
G: 204
B: 252

R: 140
G: 143
B: 248

R: 105
G: 169
B: 250

R: 179
G: 115
B: 247

Light Chamber #1

Light Chamber #2

R: 179
G: 115
B: 247

R: 255
G: 140
B: 253

R: 217
G: 127
B: 250

R: 245
G: 116
B: 205

R: 255
G: 140
B: 253

R: 229
G: 093
B: 157

Light Chamber #3

Light Chamber #4

14

16

17

16 View of west façade

17 View of south façade

18 Night view of light chamber

19 Dusk view of courtyard

Mixed-Use Tower
China World Trade Center

Beijing, China
Designed 2001–02

Taking its place among some of the tallest structures in the world, the 330-meter-tall Mega Tower is an expression of the mixed-use nature of its program, an innovative approach to efficient engineering concepts, and a desire to create a distinctive and iconic form for the city of Beijing.

Designed to integrate architecture, structural design, and mechanical systems engineering, the Mega Tower takes inspiration from one of nature's most efficient cantilevers: the bamboo plant. Fibrous on the outside, hollow on the inside, and stiffened with periodic diaphragms, bamboo serves as an organic model for the design of the ultra-tall office tower and atrium hotel. The natural formation of bamboo reveals unique structural characteristics, allowing it to behave effectively and efficiently in response to lateral loads, thereby exhibiting the genius of natural structural properties and geometric proportioning.

The geometric principles of bamboo, including the spacing of the nodes and diaphragms in addition to the diameter and culm-wall thickness, can be accurately calculated. These mathematical predictions are directly applied to the structural design of the ultra-tall tower. The superstructure consists of structural steel and composite metal deck slabs for the tower with reinforced concrete used for the low-rise and podium elements. The lateral system for the tower consists of a dual structural system combining a braced steel frame "mega-bracing" system at the exterior and a more conventional ductile movement-resisting frame at the inner layer of structure. The braced frames are laterally supported at "node" or diaphragm locations in elevation as well as at the mid-height of node locations. The structural innovation of this system allows the tower to reach great heights while introducing a new approach to tall-building design.

With Beijing's hot and cold climate, the double-skin wall provides thermal insulation and a cavity which utilizes air movement to condition different parts of the building. Sheathed by a simple outer glazing layer, the glass walls on the interior side define the office uses, hotel base, and form. Sunroom balconies within the thermal zone are proposed to mediate between the interior room environment and the outdoors.

Combining a 670-key Shangri-la Hotel and over 100,000 square meters of office uses, the tower places separate lobbies for hotel and office functions at the ground level. Active public hotel elements and restaurants are located at the lower levels, and a second-level connecting bridge and promenade leads to the Grand Ballroom in a separate building. Efficient office spaces occupy the lower and mid-tower floors. At a height of approximately 150 meters, the Shangri-la Hotel utilizes an atrium plan for 28 levels. At the base of the atrium are additional restaurants and public areas capitalizing on the dramatic space and views. Above the hotel are executive office floors and a public observation floor that will have expansive views of Beijing.

The undulating tower profile, while responding to the development of internal program spaces, also creates a simple identifiable form in the Beijing skyline. The play of sunlight or night lighting on the sloped surfaces accentuates the strong sculptural shape. The top of the building will incorporate a helipad, penthouse screen, telecommunication apparatus, and building lighting.

1 Bamboo grove
2 Alternative structural systems
3 Bamboo section
4 Building section

1

2

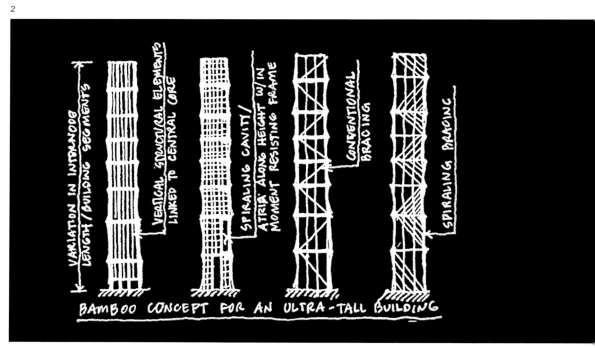

VARIATION IN INTERNODE LENGTH / BUILDING SEGMENTS

VERTICAL STRUCTURAL ELEMENTS LINKED TO CENTRAL CORE

SPIRALING CAVITY / ATRIA ALONG HEIGHT W/IN MOMENT RESISTING FRAME

CONVENTIONAL BRACING

SPIRALING BRACING

BAMBOO CONCEPT FOR AN ULTRA-TALL BUILDING

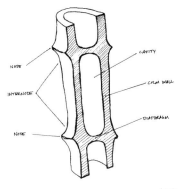

CROSS SECTION - SEGMENT OF BAMBOO STEM (CULM)

3

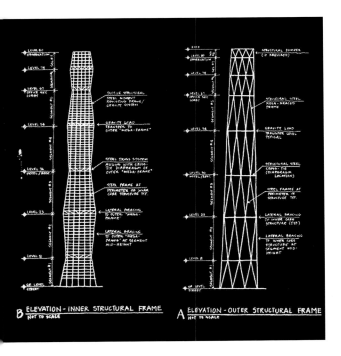

B ELEVATION - INNER STRUCTURAL FRAME
NOT TO SCALE

A ELEVATION - OUTER STRUCTURAL FRAME
NOT TO SCALE

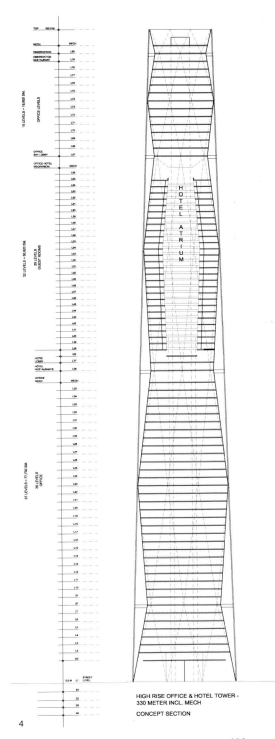

HIGH RISE OFFICE & HOTEL TOWER -
330 METER INCL. MECH

CONCEPT SECTION

4

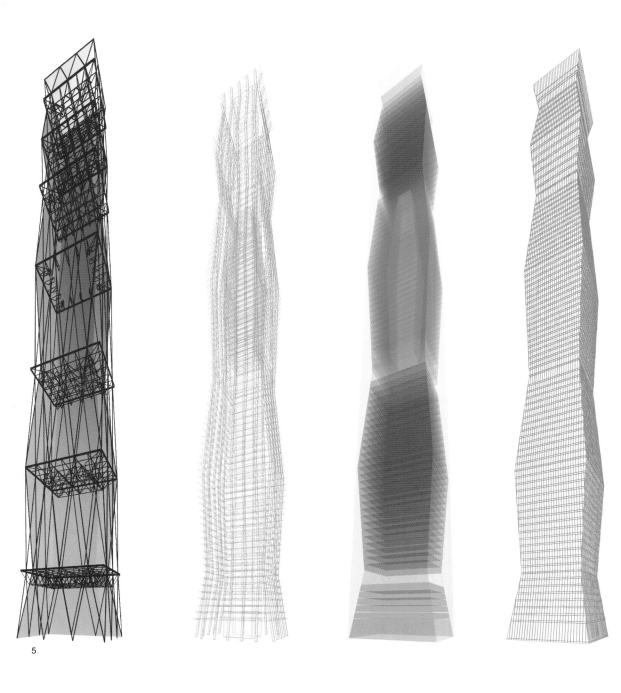

5

5 Structural and cladding components

6 View from west

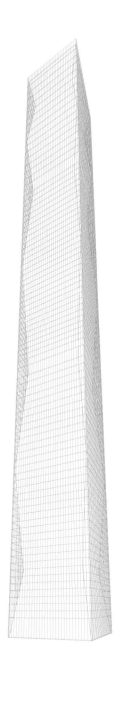

6

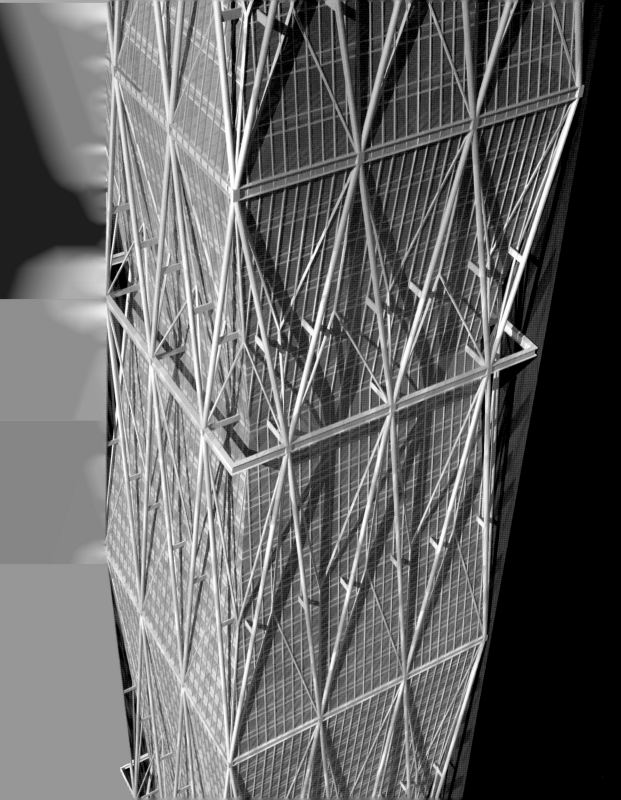

7 View of tower framing

8 Typical hotel floor plan

9 Typical office floor plan

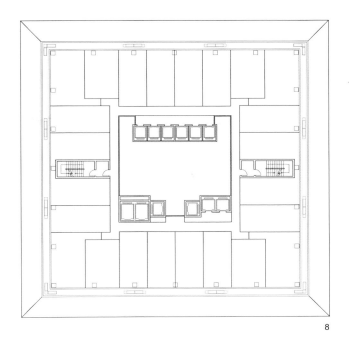

8

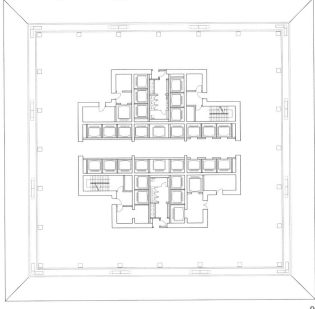

9

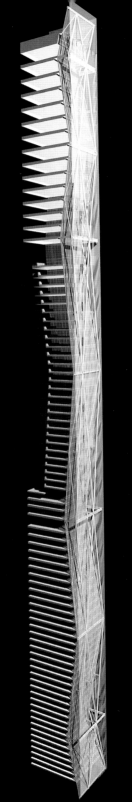

10

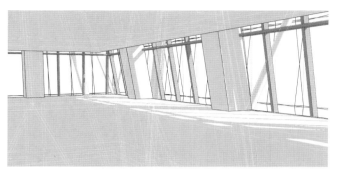

11

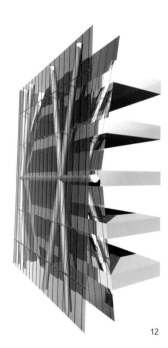

12

10 Section diagram

11 Interior view

12 Detail of cladding

13 View of tower from below

Private Residence

Bellas, Portugal
Designed 2001–02

The Jordan House is situated to the northwest of Lisbon, Portugal, in the town of Bellas, a newly established residential suburban development built around the fairways of a golf course. The area consists of undulating hills, and the house itself occupies the end of a peninsula surrounded on three sides by steep slopes.

The site is approached from a sloping road flanked by landscaped terraces and ocher limestone outcroppings. The property is accessed from the rear through a courtyard, reminiscent of traditional Portuguese entry sequences that have their origin in Moorish space organization.

A narrow entrance is formed between sloping rockery walls, compressing space. From this threshold the space expands into a walled garden—an oasis of taut manicured lawn edged by a trickling water channel. Ahead, a copper roof curves and rises from the rockery, the red-brown hues of the copper blending with the ochre-red rock. As the roof emerges, the space beneath is enclosed by glass walls that lead to a central entrance hall.

The layout of the program is greatly influenced by the differing site levels; public spaces are situated on the upper (road) level while the private and service spaces are organized on the lower (ground) level. At the center is the "pod"—a core focused on a spiral glass staircase encased by the glass shelves of the library, washed with natural light from above, and descending to a wine cellar below. Service facilities are housed within this pod; a kitchenette, servery, toilets, changing rooms, and closets. Passing through the pod around the staircase, space is again compressed until it emerges into a spacious lounge that offers panoramic views across the golf course, hills, and valleys beyond.

The exposed timber structure of the roof hovers above, stressing the continuity of the spaces below by means of radiating beams that follow the form of the roof. The pod, clad in a dark wood veneer, becomes a piece of free-standing cabinetry within the space—its curvilinear form encourages the flow of space, drawing the lounge into the dining and pool areas, uninterrupted by partitions.

The rooms of the lower level are organized in a radial pattern around the spiral staircase. The bedrooms face east, while the master bedroom is centered, facing south, offering long vistas down the valley. The kitchen, breakfast, and services areas are located on the west side. At this level, ramped driveways link the road to the garage, which takes advantage of the sloping site to embed itself in the ground.

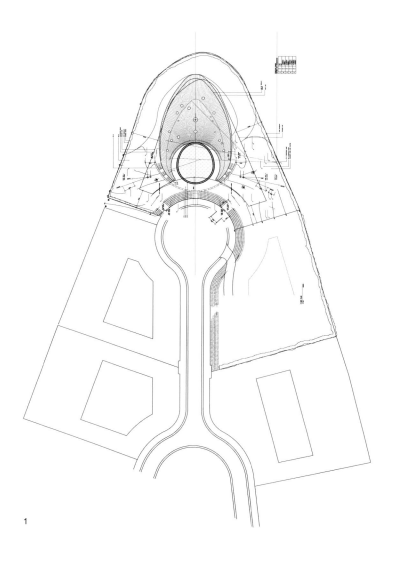

1

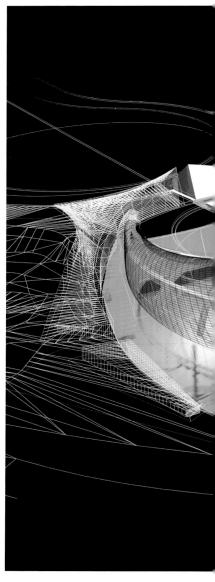

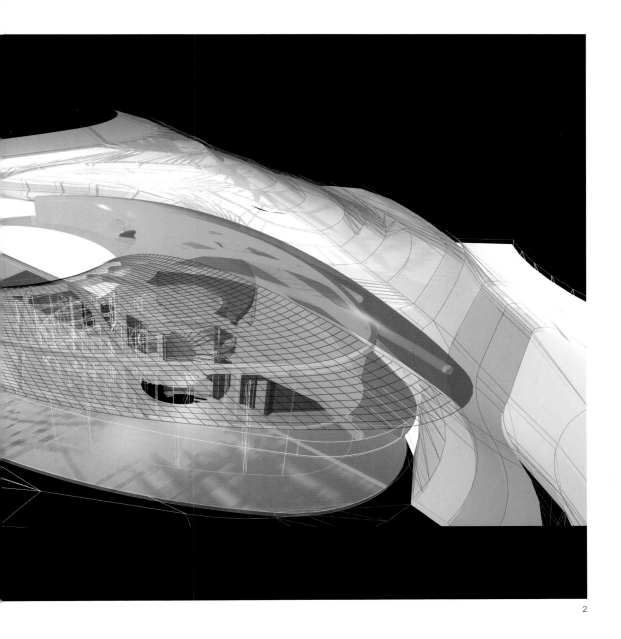

1 Site plan

2 View from southwest

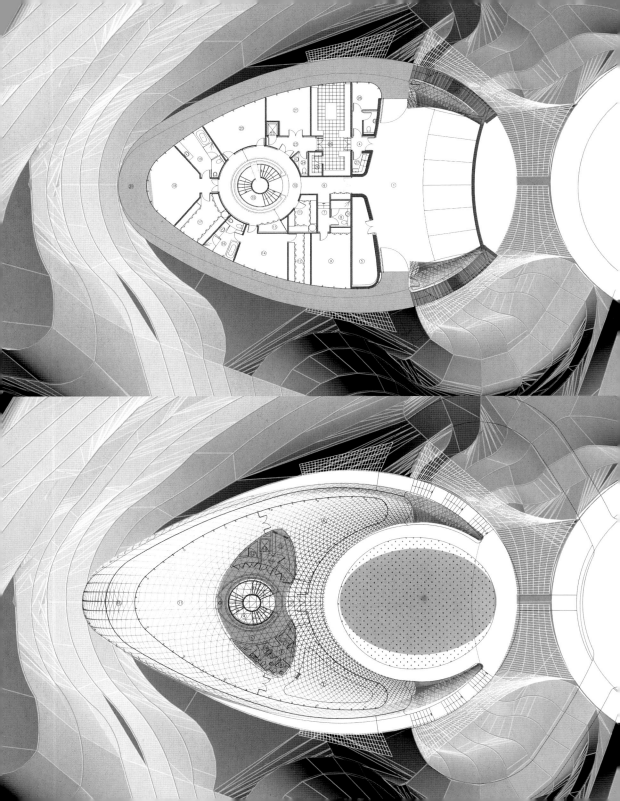

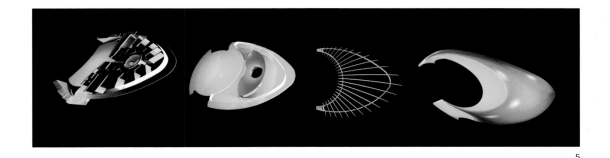

5

6

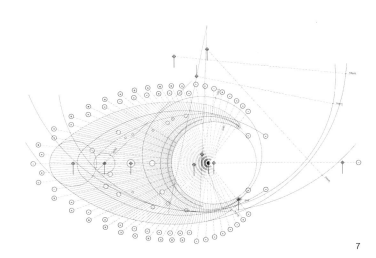

7

3 First-level plan

4 Second-level plan

5 Component diagram

6 Longitudinal section

7 Geometry diagram

8 View of entrance

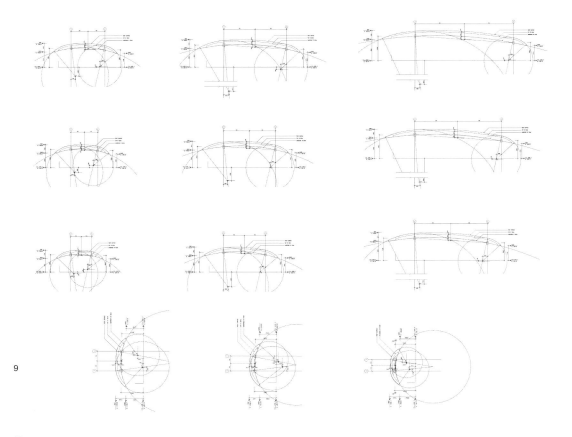

9

10

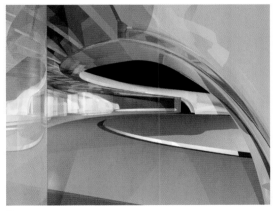

11

12

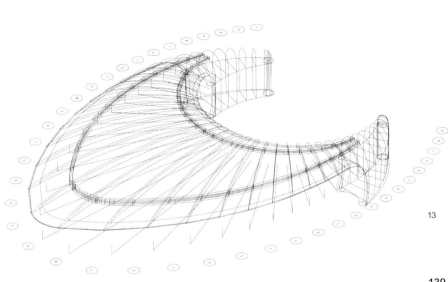

13

139

Visitor Center
Washington Monument

Designed with Diana Balmori
of Balmori Associates, Landscape Architects

Washington, D.C.
Competition 2002

The design of a new visitor center for the Washington Monument responds to an expanded program of exhibits and visitor amenities, utilizing the inhherent geometries of the monument in conjunction with axes of the Washington Mall to generate its form. The design, developed together with landscape architect Diana Balmori, incorporates additional security requirements through a composition of three low walls which enclose three tilted planes of topography. The three planes tilt at different angles: the existing horizontal circle, an elliptical form tilting at 5 degrees, and a lower elliptical form—the retaining wall—tilting at 3.5 degrees in the opposite direction. The subtle, heaving geometry of the resulting land forms creates a counterpoint to the static form of the obelisk and is achieved through a balance of cutting and filling of the existing topography which discretely integrated the new security wall while preserving the grade level at the obelisk's base. The new walls are constructed of cut Maryland Marble, the same stone used in the Monument. A glass coping at the top edge of each plane is illuminated from behind, at night creating a powerful element in the composition of monuments on the Mall.

The obelisk regains its sun-marker role through the registration of shadows on the ground plane at significant times of the year. The exhibit spaces and associated support spaces of the new visitor center exist at a below-grade level that is accessed from an opening in the tilting landforms circumnavigating the obelisk. This main entrance aligns with shadows cast by the obelisk at each equinox and at 5 P.M. on July 4, and the shadows are cast through apertures in the earth and registered as lines on the wall within the center's main circulation spine. The axis of circulation shifts to register the shift in the axis from the Capitol dome to the Lincoln Monument, resolving the two axes through the flare of the walls on either side of the center's main entrance.

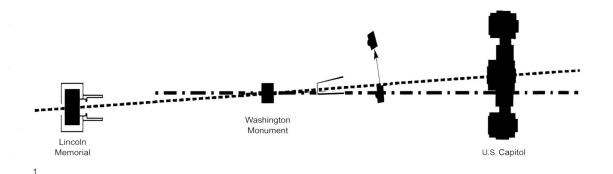

Lincoln
Memorial

Washington
Monument

U.S. Capitol

1

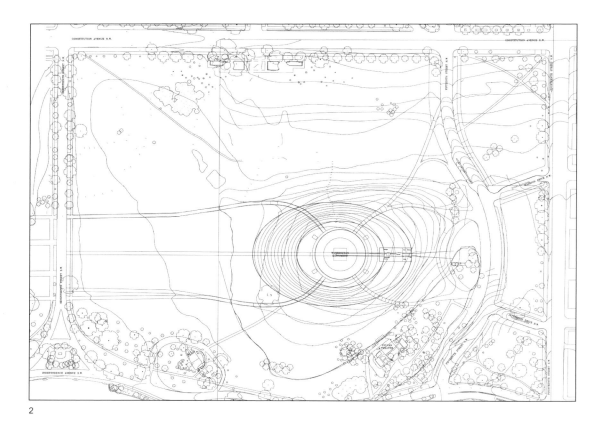

2

3

1 Diagram of axial relationship between monuments

2 Site plan

3 View of the Washington Monument

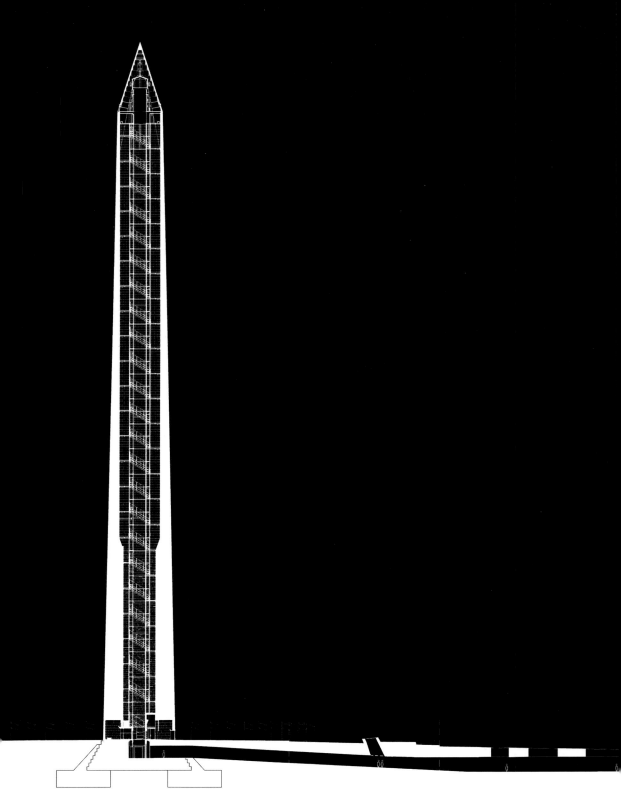

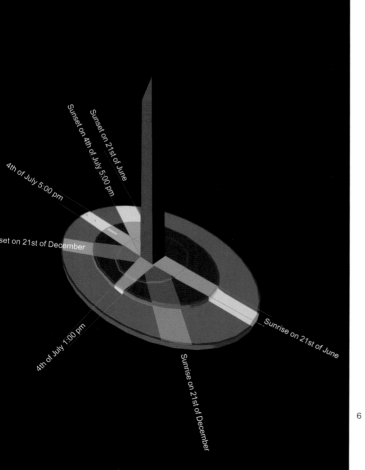

5

Sunset on 21st of June
Sunset on 4th of July 5:00 pm
4th of July 5:00 pm
set on 21st of December
4th of July 1:00 pm
Sunrise on 21st of June
Sunrise on 21st of December

6

4 Section through entry
5 Shadow diagram of elliptical berms
6 Shadow diagram of obelisk
7 Shadow movement

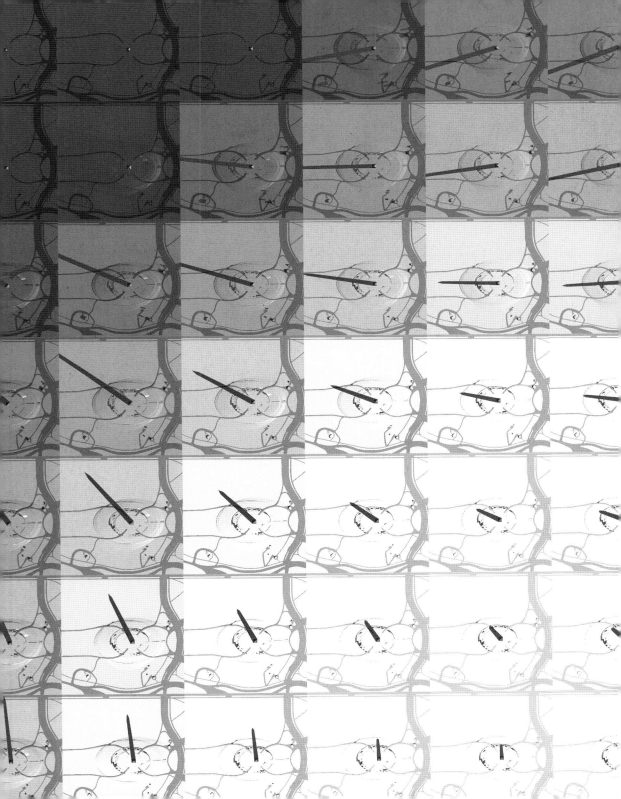

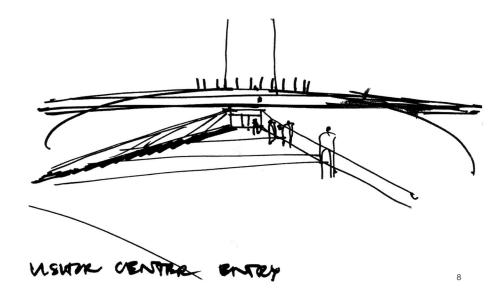

VISITOR CENTER ENTRY

8 Perspective view at entrance

9 Computer model of main components

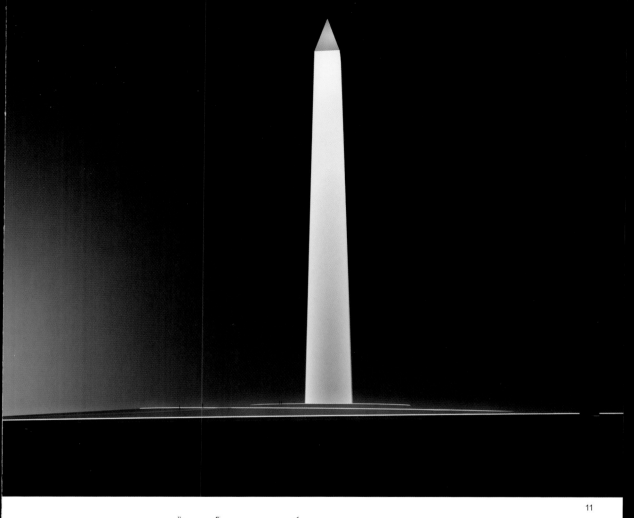

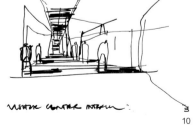

10 Perspective view at visitor center interior

11 Night view showing illuminated ellipses

12 Detail of illuminated retaining wall

13 Night view of entrance

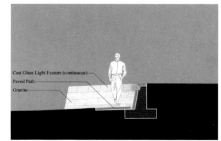

Cast Glass Light Feature (continuous)
Paved Path
Granite

Bruce Graham Interviewed by Detlef Mertins

August 7, 2002
Hobe Sound, Florida

Bruce J. Graham was born in 1925 in La Cumbre, Colombia. He studied civil engineering for two years at the Case School of Engineering before serving in the Navy during World War II. After the War, he studied architecture at the University of Pennsylvania, graduating in 1948. Graham worked for three years in the Chicago architectural firm of Holabird, Root & Burgee. He joined the Chicago office of Skidmore, Owings & Merrill in 1951 as chief of design and was elected a partner in 1960. Graham became a specialist in high-rise corporate buildings, designing skyscrapers and office complexes in Chicago and around the world. Two of Chicago's landmarks—the Sears Tower and the John Hancock Center—were designed by Graham in partnership with structural engineer Fazlur Khan. Graham retired from SOM in 1989 and now lives with his wife, Jane, in Hobe Sound, Florida. He is a member of the College of Fellows of the American Institute of Architects and an honorary member of the Royal Institute of British Architects. He continues to serve as a trustee of the University of Pennsylvania.

Detlef Mertins is Associate Professor at the University of Toronto. He has written extensively on the history of modernism in the 20th century, including essays in the catalogues for Mies in Berlin *(Museum of Modern Art) and* Mies in America *(Canadian Center for Architecture and Whitney Museum of American Art). He also has been professional advisor for several design competitions in Canada, including the Downsview Park Competition (Toronto, 1999–2000). His book* Mies: In and Against the World *is forthcoming with Phaidon Press.*

Detlef Mertins: During the forty years that you were at SOM, what would you say were the guiding principles, approaches, or ideas for your architecture?

Bruce Graham: Most important was working in Chicago, which I think is still the best architectural city in the United States. It gave you direction, an overall direction. I don't mean that you had to imitate other architects like Frank Lloyd Wright, Louis Sullivan, or even Mies. But there was a great tradition in architecture and a city that was perfectly planned after the big fire. It has a grid and a beach that goes all the way from Indiana to Milwaukee. The grid created a sense of direction for the people. It created neighborhoods with their own parks, their own school systems, and so on. I followed that kind of philosophy.

DM: So you inherited an architectural tradition and a body of work that you saw as a positive influence, something that you had to respond to. And the city itself was important as a guide.

BG: In what other city would the businessmen elect an architect to be assistant chairman of the Central Area Committee? Can you imagine New York doing that? Forget it. Or Los Angeles?

DM: You've mentioned a number of architects: Wright, Sullivan, and Mies. In things you've written, you've highlighted the importance of the expression of structure, which is certainly part of the legacy of those architects. How do you see yourself contributing to that Chicago theme?

BG: Let me describe the difference between my idea of architecture and a lot of other architects. Number one, architecture is not painting or sculpture. Archi-

tecture is much more like music, which has an element of time. Architecture is about space and movement. It's four-dimensional. I learned that very early when I went to Chartres Cathedral. I walked up the hill and found the square and then the church and walked in, and this fantastic space opened up. There was a funeral, and they were playing Mozart's unfinished *Requiem*. I had to cry. Moving through that space with that music was unbelievable. Space is what architecture is all about. Not only interior but also exterior. And the movement of people. That's true whether you go to Greece, or to Karnak, or to any other place and see any other great architecture of the past. I believe that modern architecture should do the same. In Chicago our advantage was that we had engineers. Structure is still essential to the creation of space, just as it was in Chartres Cathedral.

DM: How do you work with a structure architecturally? How do you work on a structural idea?
BG: Each structure depends on the kind of building you're making. The spaces depend on the intended uses. A church is different from an office building.

DM: Did you work closely with engineers?
BG: Absolutely. When Bill Hartman took over the SOM office, it was the first thing that I pushed for. We were very lucky to get some very good engineers, especially Fazlur Khan. We had an older engineer at first, who was very nice and very good. But when we wanted to put the columns for the Inland Steel Building on the outside in order to have a clear space inside, he said, "I can't do it. But there's a young engineer at the University of Illinois." So Faz came over, and we did it. From then on, Faz and I were buddies.

DM: What was it like working with Fazlur Khan? What was the exchange like between you?
BG: Obviously, it was different every time. We didn't have the same discussions each time. But I would have a sketch or an idea, and then Faz would come, and we'd talk about what the structure would be like. We also talked to a very good mechanical engineer who worked with us. Faz trained more engineers and put together a team of excellent people. Then we di-

vided the office into studios that were relatively separate. Each studio had a senior architect or design partner directing it, with a managing partner as well. Each team had mechanical engineers and structural engineers working directly with them. It was as if each was a little office rather than there being one big office. The intimacy and the relationships within the studios were terrific.

DM: Did you ever want to pursue an architectural idea that seemed illogical to Faz structurally?
BG: Not me. I was very involved in engineering. In fact, before I studied architecture, I took engineering and applied sciences.

DM: Even Mies, in some instances, stretched the logic of structure. The roof of the New National Gallery is probably the most well-known case. The structure is being stressed in order to achieve the effect of levitation that he wanted.
BG: Well, I love the museum. It's a wonderful gallery. But you're right. Mies wasn't oriented to engineering, although he admired engineers.

DM: And he worked with engineers. Myron Goldsmith was very important for his understanding of structure.
BG: Myron was an architect-engineer. He was an architect first. Faz was a real engineer.

DM: What's the difference?
BG: The sophistication.

DM: You once said that Mies's approach to the expression of structure was aesthetic. What did you mean by that?

BG: He was fantastic with the proportion of space and making structure as an expression of it. In most cases, it was beautifully done. There's no question that he was a master of architecture. When he put mullions in front of the columns at 860 Lake Shore Drive, he called it structural, but he meant aesthetic structure, not Bruce Graham or Faz Khan structure. He meant the aesthetic structure that keeps the rhythm of the building as a whole.

DM: How was Mies significant for your work?

BG: He was significant, but Chicago architecture is a broader historical thing. It isn't just Mies. It isn't just one person. Louis Sullivan wasn't exactly stupid. The structures of Louis Sullivan are also very clear, very clearly expressed. By the way, that's why I went to Holabird & Root first, before I went to SOM. They had a tradition of doing structural engineering and architecture together.

DM: Wasn't it also Mies who suggested that you do that?

BG: Yes. When I was a student, I came from Philadelphia to see him. He received me. He was a very nice man, a very simple man. I asked him where I should go to work, and he said Holabird & Root.

DM: What else did you talk about with Mies?

BG: We were good friends. There wasn't another intellect like him in the city. There just wasn't. The person I didn't like, as a person, was Frank Lloyd Wright. He was a real son of a bitch. I gave him hell one time. He was giving a speech at the University of Chicago and was blasting me. So I finally got up and said, "Mr. Wright, why don't you sit down and shut up?" And I walked out. It's ridiculous for an architect to criticize another architect that way. But by that time, he was a little insane. He certainly wasn't a constructivist. Fallingwater nearly collapsed. He wouldn't listen.

DM: Did you see Mies as a constructivist?

BG: Yes.

DM: What did you talk about with him?

BG: How the wine was. Once in his old apartment—he had an easy chair with a table and his cigars and his martini and all the furniture against the wall—somebody asked him why he didn't move into 860 Lake Shore Drive. He said, "There's no place to put the furniture. I was born in a little village in Germany. I can dream and imagine this new world, but I can't live in it."

DM: Mies said that he wasn't working on architecture but on architecture as a language. Did you see yourself working on a language? If so, how?

BG: Yes. Around the Chicago area and the Middle West there was a vocabulary that I felt very strongly. But when you build in other cities, like Nashville, Tennessee, or Cincinnati, Ohio, you don't just plunk in a Chicago building. You try to see what the city's character is and express it. It was the same with the build-

ings I did in London and Barcelona. Still, the structure was important. Let me tell you about Bishopsgate in the Broadgate Development in London. The structural steel there was treated with a paint that lasts forever and fireproofs the steel. It was invented by Sears Roebuck but hasn't been allowed in the United States, until very recently when it was used in Texas. We lobbied to use it in Chicago and other places because it makes such a big difference. The character of the steel is much clearer.

DM: Your practice was national and international in scope, but you were very attuned to the specific aspects of the place in which you were working. I wonder if you could speak a little more about that. What did you seek to understand about a place when you came to work in it?

BG: Well, Barcelona is a good example. They had a fantastic mayor, by the way. He understood the city, and the city had a special character with a long tradition. When you do a modern building in a place like that, you still want it to fit in. I think I achieved that with the hotel I designed there. At least the ex-Prime Minister of England thought so. She bought an apartment on the fortieth floor. You have to look at the character of the city. In Hong Kong I would do a different kind of hotel than in Chicago. The same way with any other place.

DM: Were you also interested in how construction varies from one place to another?

BG: That's right. There was no way you could build a structural-steel tower in Egypt. Forget it.

DM: You have a certain fondness for the courtyard house, I believe. Your own house in Chicago was a courtyard house. How is it that, as a modern architect, you were drawn to that vernacular type?

BG: Well, remember, I was raised in Peru, and all the houses in the nice neighborhoods in Peru, and the ancient ones, had courtyards. The beauty of a courtyard in a city is, number one, safety. Number two, it has spaces that you can decorate and separate from the road. There's a sense of privacy that you don't get with a regular house.

DM: Since your work varies in relation to the specific conditions of a local place, how would you describe the continuities from one project to the next?

BG: Certainly the most important thing in architecture is space—

DM: Regardless of where you're building, you want to find a way to create spatial experiences.

BG: That's right.

DM: And regardless of what kind of construction you're using, you want to articulate that, to make a clear structure.

BG: You got it.

DM: Let's talk a little bit about some other building types. For a while you were exploring the potentials of tubular structure for your high-rise buildings. You made a series of projects that are essays on this idea—from the Brunswick Building (Chicago, 1965) to One Shell Plaza (Houston, 1972) and the Sears Tower (Chicago, 1974). Incidentally, that's a wonderful maquette of the Sears Tower that you have. How did you go about working with that type of structure?

BG: Well, the tubular structure was a basic idea for a very tall building. A frame building doesn't have the same capacity and economy that a tubular building does. It's a very simple way to build structures, putting the strength of the building on the exterior with the spans towards the core. In that way, the space in between can be free for various uses, which is particularly important in office buildings. Everybody thinks they were very expensive, but they weren't. The Sears Tower and Hancock Center (Chicago, 1970) were not expensive.

DM: It's interesting that those buildings are all quite different from one another, despite using the same structural idea. What motivated the differences? Why not just repeat the idea more directly each time?

BG: Because an office building is not the same as an apartment building. The Hancock Center was a mixed-use building. The different needs of the various uses suggested the taping shape. One Shell Plaza was originally going to be in Cor-Ten steel but we thought to reserve that for the Richard J. Daley Center (Chicago, 1965) which faced it across the plaza.

DM: Were you interested in developing or refining anything architecturally?

BG: The main thing was that the structure define space.

DM: What determined the difference in expression between the Brunswick Building and One Shell Plaza?

BG: Money.

DM: Another architectural idea that recurs in your work is the open framework or structural cage. There's something of this already, but in a Miesian way, at Kimberly-Clark (Neeham, Wisconsin, 1956) and then more fully at the Business Men's Assurance (Kansas City, Missouri, 1964). Later, The Terraces at Perimeter Center (Atlanta, 1986) is a very exuberant demonstration and there were a number of others in between.

BG: Well, it depended on the uses of the building. Kimberly-Clark is a low-rise building and therefore we want to keep the structure very simple and to express the spaces inside. For example, the headquarters part is different from the overall office building. Up in Wisconsin, it seemed appropriate to look down to the lake and let the landscape come into the building. It was a country building, not a city building. There's a relationship there with the landscape.

The same thing is true at the Upjohn Building (Kalamazoo, Michigan, 1961). It's the relationship of the

landscape to the building. At the Sears Tower, for instance, you can't have the landscaping that you can have out in the country.

DM: So the cage buildings are about being open to the landscape. Would you explain a little bit more how the studio system works? How many people would be in a studio?

BG: It depends on the size of the project. A team generally consisted of about fifteen people. Then there was an interior design group as well. They were separate but would work with the architectural team on the interior design. Architects don't tend to be masters of the layout of furniture.

DM: So the teams would come up with a comprehensive vision, including the interiors and the selection of art.

BG: There was always a design partner in charge of a studio project. Always. He might be working with two or three different teams on two or three different projects.

DM: How did the studio system come into being?

BG: It started relatively early when Bill Hartman took over the SOM office in Chicago. We had studios then

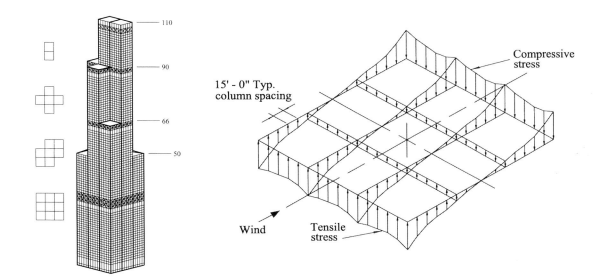

110

90

66

50

15' - 0" Typ.
column spacing

Compressive
stress

Wind

Tensile
stress

that were a little different than the ones that evolved later. But still, it was somewhat the same idea.

DM: How did Myron Goldsmith fit into the system?
BG: He came to us from California with another fellow. They needed jobs, so I hired them. I was doing a hotel near the downtown and the other guy kept criticizing it, telling me how bad it was. Finally Walter Peterhans—you know he taught with Mies at the Illinois Institute of Technology—came over and told him to shut up. That was the end of that. Myron later became a partner.

DM: Did Myron have his own studio?
BG: Well, the teams weren't necessarily tied to one partner. He was teaching part of the time and didn't do as much work as I did.
DM: Is it true that in the early days at SOM design credit wasn't given to partners for specific projects? As I understand it, Nat Owings wanted the firm to be known as a firm more than for its individual designers.
BG: At one point, individual partners started to get credit. Walter Netsch got credit for the University of Illinois, and then I got credit for the Sears Tower.

DM: Was getting credit important to you?
BG: No. I regret that things changed. It was a tradition. And, besides, everyone knew, for instance, that Gordon Bunshaft was a certain architect in New York. Incidentally, he was the best architect in the New York office by far.

DM: How well did you know him? What was your relationship like?
BG: We were friends, but we never worked together because we were far apart. I admired him, and he liked my work. He wished he could do some buildings in Chicago instead of just in New York. In New York, do you see a building that looks better than Lever House? Forget it. That's the best looking building in New York. Gordon was a very good architect, and he was very nice. He built all over the world, in Europe, and I got to know him very well. We were close friends.

DM: He was an art collector, wasn't he?
BG: I'll say. He was a very good friend of a lot of artists. Well, I was too.

DM: Who did you know? Whose work did you use in your projects?

BG: Alexander Calder was a very good friend of mine, and I used Henry Moore quite a lot. Calder was a character, but he was phenomenal—a wonderful guy, a great artist, and a terrific sense of humor. When he was a student at the University of Pennsylvania he got interested in how to help starving people around the world. He went to the Cleveland Clinic Hospital and learned a lot about that. Then, after the War, he went to Johns Hopkins University.

DM: What appealed to you about his work?
BG: It was simply beautiful. Calder and Moore were also very responsive to architecture and urbanism. Unlike Picasso. The same with Joan Miró. He's a terrific person. I would talk with him in Spanish.

Do you know the story behind the Picasso in Chicago? There were three firms working on the Daley Center, and the others all wanted to make a Miesian building. I talked them out of it and into the big span, since it was a court building and you needed to express the larger spaces. One day Bill Hartman took a vote on who should be the artist. One person said Henry Moore, the second said Henry Moore, the third said Henry Moore. I said Pablo Picasso, and Bill said, "Picasso wins." Then it went to the mayor, and the mayor said, "Bill, if you say so we'll do it." Bill went to Picasso and asked him if he would do a sculpture. He made a maquette. When Bill brought it back, I said, "Bill, it's too small. It just doesn't relate to the building." So we went back to Picasso, and he was delighted.

He made a huge maquette, and then the mayor said, "How much money does he want, Bill?" Bill said, "He didn't say." So the mayor made out a check for two million dollars. Bill took it to Picasso, came back, and the mayor said, "Did he take the check?" "He tore it up." "Does he want more money?" "He doesn't want any money." The mayor said, "Why not?" "Because Chicago is the only city that had ever asked him to do a civic sculpture." So he did it for nothing.

When Henry Moore and Miró both heard about that, they decided to also donate the sculptures they were doing for the city. Henry Moore did a big one that's now in the Art Institute of Chicago. Artists like to be involved in urban architecture. After all, what could be more important?

One time I did a building in Wichita, Kansas. I asked Calder if he would do a mobile in the big space. Because the poor city didn't have any squares, I made the building with a glass corner. He said he would and came to Wichita with six different maquettes. He asked them to choose one. Of course, they ended up choosing the right one. Then he told the city, "Okay, you can have all the others too." He gave them all free of charge to the University. Artists don't give a damn about money.

DM: I believe you were a painter yourself at one point.
BG: When I was at the University of Pennsylvania, studying architecture, I did painting and sculpture, and was quite good.

DM: Did that inform your architecture in any way?
BG: Not really. The Beaux-Arts professors of that time insisted that all the architects learn to paint and do sculpture. They were right. Then, when you make drawings to express your building, you know something about drawing.

DM: Did you collect art?
BG: I've got about six Calders, all of which he gave me. We've also got a Henry Moore, some Peruvian pre-Columbian work, and some pieces by the Croatian Rovenj Grisa.

DM: Let's talk a little bit about interiors and furniture. Did you subscribe to the idea of total design?

BG: In some cases, like the Upjohn Building. Jane Abend, who later became my wife, designed a lot of the furniture, because it's a very private kind of office building owned by a family. That's one case where total design makes sense. But at the Sears Tower there are a million tenants, and everyone is going to need their own design. By then Jane and I were married, and she was no longer working at SOM. She did the interiors for some law firms there. There are some very good interior designers at SOM and also outside of SOM.

DM: Were you ever tempted to design furniture yourself? Did you want to work at that scale?
BG: No.

DM: Why?
BG: I was quite happy with Mies chairs, so why should I get into that? Just buy a Mies chair.

DM: Let's go back now to talk a little bit more about the city and urbanism. You once said that SOM was more involved in making cities, that you were more interested in building cities than in building buildings.
BG: Building parts of cities. I didn't think that each building should be a temple. Rather it should be part of the whole city. The relationship between buildings is very important to me.

DM: You've spoken out against aspects of modern urbanism, against expressways and sprawl. What can an architect do about infrastructure and development at that scale?
BG: We could have done much more for Chicago if the governor hadn't killed the expressway program, which called for the following: when you come from the airport to the city, it's terrible. All the trucks have to come downtown. With Mayor Daly, we agreed that the trucks should go around the city and not come downtown and then go on to Indiana. I don't know if you ever heard of Joe Passenau. He was a professor of planning in St. Louis and was part of SOM for a while. I asked Joe to help us with this, and he did a terrific job. The neighborhoods loved it. They loved the way our road was graded so there would be no noise into

the neighborhood. Then the governor killed the program. They should still do it.

DM: Did you subscribe to the modernist idea of doing away with streets, as Le Corbusier argued?
BG: He was French. Just go to France and see the mess it is now—sadly, unfortunately.

DM: What kind of contribution can architects make to urbanism?
BG: In Chicago, different firms used to meet and talk about the city and what it needed. We used to have meetings in which the businessmen would come and listen to us. I think the whole of the South Side was started by a Chicago architect.

DM: You're clearly very conversant with the economics and politics of urban development. It's interesting that in your recollections you often focus on those things.
BG: Historically, it was always that way. Why were the great cathedrals built? Not because an architect wanted to build them but because the power of the church wanted to build them. It was the result of a political motive or social movement. As an architect you have to be aware of that and express it.

DM: Do you see the architect, then, as someone who participates in a larger conversation with all of those people, as someone who takes up the issues of the day and contributes to things that people are thinking about from many other perspectives?
BG: Yes, that's true. Architects should do that. I mean, that was the whole idea of the Bauhaus. That's what it was all about.

DM: When you're working on a specific site, designing a building or a complex of buildings for it, how do you think of its larger urban implications?
BG: It was one of the strengths of Chicago that the architects shared a vernacular with which to build the city. You can't say that of New York or San Francisco.

DM: Did SOM have planners working in the firm?
BG: Yes.

DM: Were they part of the studios in the same way that the engineers were?
BG: They had a separate group, but they would work on each project with each team just like an engineer would be part of the team.

DM: Do you think there are differences between modernism in America and in Europe?
BG: Yes. In London, I felt you had to integrate modern buildings into the historical character of the city. That would be true of most cities in Europe. In Chicago, there was virtually nothing there to start with except a lake and a city plan by Daniel Burnham. That was true of America as a whole. Now it's become a little different. As time passes, some cities have developed a character, which is very satisfactory, in my mind. Minnesota is very different than Chicago and has some very nice buildings. Milwaukee is very different than Chicago. Even the Midwest has a certain kind of unity, but the East Coast doesn't.
A few cities like Philadelphia have preserved their character. I'm a trustee of the University of Pennsylvania, and Gary Hack, who's a planner and the Dean of the Graduate School of Fine Arts, has done a terrific job of planning around the University itself. He's now been appointed to head the planning commission for the City of Philadelphia. That kind of thing is unusual. When I went to school there, all the wealthy people lived in the suburbs because the downtown was so bad. That's turned around. The character of the city is preserved, and the city is safer and easier to use.

DM: What was your experience there as a student?
BG: I liked it. My brother was going to medical school there. I like Philadelphia. I like the university. You could study in many other fields too. History, for instance, was terrific, and you could go to the engineering school.

DM: I understand that as a student you were outspoken at times. What was going on then that you didn't like?
BG: The students were very disgusted with our teachers at Penn. Some of them were old-fashioned and didn't understand modern architecture. They also talked to

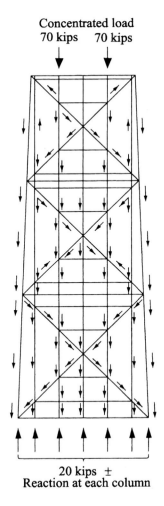

Concentrated load
70 kips   70 kips

20 kips ±
Reaction at each column

us as if we were children. Many of us were GIs and so were older. I had already gone to the Case School of Engineering and knew something about building. Dr. Roth, who taught history at Penn, was terrific. I really learned a lot from him, but not from others. The whole school was dissatisfied, so the administration did a review and brought some new faculty in, including Holmes Perkins. That's when Kahn really got involved.

DM: What kind of work did you do as a student? Was it modernist or traditional?
BG: Modernist. We still had the old École des Beaux-Arts system, but it was then abandoned, not just at Penn but at all the other schools too.

DM: Did you have any experiences with Louis Kahn? Was he of any importance to you?
BG: Yes, I did. He was a very generous man and, I thought, a fantastic architect. Oskar Stonorov from his office asked me to work there. For three weeks, I helped with some drawings, for nothing. In those days, students did that. Mies used to pay a dollar an hour. He was very generous.

DM: Let's go back to the question of urbanism. One of the challenges facing architects today is how to design big buildings within existing cities and achieve new architectural ideas. How did you approach that problem in your time?

163

BG: That's a complicated question because I don't think it applies everywhere. In Chicago, the power of the original plan makes a hell of a difference. The problem with a lot of cities is that they never made such a plan. Then all of a sudden, when they have to begin to put bigger things in, they don't fit. The streets aren't laid out right. New York is a very good example. In my mind, as urban planning, it stinks. It doesn't have any personality, character, public spaces, recreational spaces, nothing, zero. Except for Central Park. That's the only thing they have. There hasn't been anything along the shore until recently. And the relationship between buildings is not at all sympathetic. In Florida, there's also no planning. They had a great chance to build beautiful cities, and they blew it. It's just totally out of control, just driven by money. They don't build public spaces. They don't build avenues. They don't build locations for the arts. They don't even take advantage of the beaches in this state.

I don't know if you know the little church I did on the south side of Chicago. There was a wonderful priest whose supportive attitude transformed an entire neighborhood. He asked me to do a church because part of their building was collapsing. There was a school behind the church where two fabulous nuns taught the kids. This priest was really effective in keeping the kids away from drugs. It was a poor black neighborhood, and about 90 percent of the students went on to college. The school had a perfect record with the kids. Imagine that in any other place. So I said, "Sure, I'll do the church," and I got Chicagoans to contribute the money. He didn't have to put up a nickel.

DM: You've mentioned other examples of that kind of generosity. What are your thoughts about an architect's social responsibilities? A firm like SOM works primarily for specific clients on specific sites—corporate clients, developers, and institutions. Do you think that there are social and political responsibilities that go beyond serving your immediate clients?

BG: Absolutely. I was a member of Central Area Committee in Chicago. If you don't engage with all those people, you won't know anything about your city, and they won't understand anything about architecture.

DM: In Chicago, then, was there a dialogue?

BG: That's the word, yes. As the Central Area Committee, we criticized Northwestern University for not having a campus in the downtown. They had the whole thing up in Evanston, so the students had to drive all the way up to the North Shore to go to university. It was ridiculous, because the central system of Chicago is so perfect. You can take the L and you're downtown. So they changed it and moved it. Northwestern's Medical School shot up in quality after that.

DM: You were instrumental, I believe, in starting the SOM Foundation and the Institute.

BG: I had partners and associate partners, too, who shared in that.

DM: How did the partners get together to create the Foundation, given that they operated so independently on their projects?

BG: The Foundation was national and involved Bunshaft, Hartman, Owings, John Merrill, and others. We had a committee, and it created the Foundation. I don't know whether they still have the committee.

DM: Do you have a favorite among all your buildings?

BG: I don't think about it that way. One of the last buildings that I enjoyed a lot was the hotel in Barcelona. The mayor, as I said, was an absolutely wonderful man who was doing a great job. He took all the parks of Barcelona and turned them over to the people. He gave them the tools to make them right. He got artists from all over the world to contribute sculptures for these little parks. People there became very proud.

When I did the hotel, Frank Gehry, who was a friend of mine, wanted to do something with the passage to the sea, from the hotel all the way to the ocean. I said sure. So Frank tried this and that, and finally he tried a fish. We went to Barcelona for a meeting and Frank was about to open the box with his model in it and the mayor said, "Wait a minute. Why don't you open Bruce's maquette first?" It included the whole project, everything, and had a fish with the same form as Frank's. So Frank said, "Oh!" Then I said, "Frank, of course, we'll use your fish." The fish that's there now was designed by Frank Gehry. Afterwards, he gave me the maquette, which I still own. By the way, I don't think he's an architect. He used to be. He designed beautiful houses along the waterfront in California. Then he took up a sculptural mode.

DM: You don't think that's architecture?
BG: Architecture is space.

DM: But what about the inside of his buildings?
BG: That's what bothers me about them. He doesn't give spaces. Who wants to be inside the stomach of a fish? I still like Frank. We're good friends.

DM: Now that there's been a resurgence of modern design around the world, do you think any of the post-modern criticisms from the 70s and 80s were justified?
BG: There are good architects and bad architects, and fortunately Chicago had a lot of good architects, which helped. But not all cities did. That's sad but true.

DM: How did you react to post-modernism?
BG: When I was in the office, there was no post-modernism. Zero.

DM: Wouldn't you have to acknowledge though that some of your later work, especially in London, included historical references? Didn't you say before how important it was for a building to fit into its urban context?
BG: In the middle of a city, especially an old city, you want the building to fit in, by means of space and relationships. Obviously as society advances, technol-ogy changes and people change, but you can still make a new building fit in. Our building in Barcelona does that pretty well. Remember that Franco hated Barcelona and treated the Catalans terribly. But Barcelona retained its integrity, even through all that. Now it's *the* city in Spain, without a doubt. I always liked Chicago for the same reason, because there was a certain integrity about the city, regardless of the architect. It's about having a vocabulary and a character. The character of the people in Chicago was totally different than the character of people in New York. Totally different. It was an industrial city. We made things, we grew things. The city related to the landscape and to the farms west and north of Chicago. All of that integrity made for the architecture of Chicago.

DM: You weren't born in Chicago, but when you came there you made it your city. As an outsider, do you feel that you could see things that Chicagoans might not have seen?
BG: I don't know why, but certainly I felt a connection with the city. I came there as a kid with a scholarship to go to university in Dayton. Then later, when the War started, I joined the Navy. I met Americans from all over. The Pacific, the sailors, and training camps . . . I went through Chicago in the Navy, going along the Great Lakes, and I always loved the city. I thought it was beautiful. After the War, I was a different person. A lot of my friends had been killed. Then I went to the University of Pennsylvania. After that, I went back to Chicago. I talked to Mies, went to Holabird & Root . . . and the rest is history.

Project Update
Terminal 3 Building
Changi International Airport, Singapore

The Changi Airport Terminal 3 project was exhibited in the 2002 Biennale in Venice, Italy. A detailed scale model representing nine structural bays of the roof replicated the floating effect of the multiple layers of louvers.

The construction of the Terminal in Singapore is proceeding. A full-size mockup of a typical structural bay, measuring 15 by 15 meters, has been built to test the effectiveness of the louver system. The terminal will be able to operate during the day without artificial illumination, using the louvers to precisely control the amount of daylight allowed into the space (the louvers are wide open during overcast weather and closed under clear skies). The louver actuators are now being tested for durability.

Rendering of terminal space

Model of six typical roof bays exhibited at the Biennale in Venice

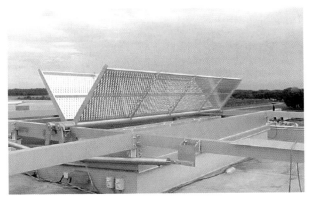

Mockup of a typical skylight

Mockup of typical 15-meter bay

Project Credits

**Automated People Mover Station
Washington Dulles International
Airport**
Chantilly, Virginia
Designed 2000–01

client
Metropolitan Washington Airports
Authority
design partner
David M. Childs
managing partner
Anthony Vacchione
planning partner
Marilyn Taylor
senior designer
Peter Ruggiero
team
Tim Dumbleton, Nicole Robertson, Mark
Leininger, Erik Boehlo, John Dosier,
Sophie Frank, Boerries Goetsch, Virginia
Harper, Peter Lefkowitz, Alissa Marquez,
Carmen Roig, Richard Shearer,
Jacqueline Suozzi, Carlos Infantes, Peter
Costanzo, Steven Danielpour, Gene
Cheek, Jonathan Barrick, Rebecca
Bascom, Holly Carson, Jennifer Chan,
Eduardo Dans, Lauren Freiman, Danielle
Hircay, William Hulver, Mi-Yeon Kim,
Clement Krug, Laura King, Ralph
Michele, Omar Myers, Ivan Nedeltchev,
Cametrick Nesmith, Traci Nottingham,
Christopher Peterson, Carlton Prime,
Lucinda Rudge, Robert Shaw, Justino
Vega
project managers
Paul Auguste, Susanne Churchill
technical coordinators
Kevin Peters, Marc Igou, Raymond
Hidalgo, Andrew Makin
structural engineering
Amman & Whitney
mechanical engineering
HC YU and Associates

**Central Plant Building
The University of California at Merced**
Designed 2001–02

client
The University of California at Merced
design partner
Craig Hartman
managing partner
Gene Schnair
planning partner
John Kriken
senior designer
Michael Duncan
team
Masis Mesropian, Mason Miller,
Ann Shih, Henry Vlanin
project manager
Jack Parker
technical coordinator
Tom McMillan
structural engineering
Peter Lee, David Inlow, Arup
mechanical engineering
Arup
landscape architect
Peter Walker and Partners

Concert Hall
Lincoln Center
New York, New York
Designed 2002

client
New York Philharmonic, Lincoln Center
collaborating team
Roger Duffy, Leigh Breslau, James
Turrell, Scott Duncan, Ursula Schneider,
Michael Brewster, Bob Arko (IDEO),
Adam Tihany, Christopher McCready,
Thomas Kerwin

Science, Math, and Technology Center
Deerfield Academy
Deerfield, Massachusetts
Designed 2001–02

client
Deerfield Academy
design partner
Roger Duffy with David M. Childs
managing partner
Anthony Vacchione
senior designers
Ursula Schneider, Scott Kirkham
collaborating artist
James Turrell
observational astronomer
Richard Walker
team
Alexandra Cuber, Vivian Lee,
Thomas Behr
project manager
Chris McCready
technical coordinator
Reiner Bagnato
structural engineering
Le Messurier
mechanical engineering
Ove Arup
landscape architect
Brown Sardina
visionary symposium participants
Richard Bonanno, physicist
Huston Eubank, green architect
Suzanne Flynt, historian
Michael Govan, director Dia Center
Kimberle Koile, comp. scientist M.I.T.
Jeffry Louis, trustee DA
Richard Little, geologist
Inigo Manglano-Ovalle, artist
James Turrell, artist
Richard Walker, astronomer
Eric Widmer, historian

Elementary School Number 11
Fairfield, Connecticut
Designed 2001–02

client
Town of Fairfield
design partner
Roger Duffy
managing partner
Anthony Vacchione
educational specialist
Walter Smith
senior designer
Scott Duncan
team
Carlo Balestri, Woong Yang,
Thibaut DeGryse, Dai-yi Oh,
Nina Roschonkowska, Ana Bravo,
Andrew Hayes, Fe Rodriguez
project manager
Chris McCready
structural engineering
DiBlasi Associates
mechanical engineering
Altieri Sebor Wieber
landscape architect
Brown Sardina

Academic Building
Greenwich Academy
Greenwich, Connecticut
Completed 2002

Mixed-Use Tower
China World Trade Center
Beijing, China
Designed 2001–02

Private Residence
Bellas, Portugal
Designed 2001–02

client
Greenwich Academy, Greenwich,
Connecticut
design partner
Roger Duffy
collaborating artist
James Turrell
managing partner
Peter Magill
educational specialist
Walter Smith
senior designer
Scott Kirkham
team
Marie-Christine Bellon Manzi, Thibaut
DeGryse, Nayyareen Chhapra, Jon Mark
Capps, Javier Haddad Conde
project manager
Christopher McCready
structural engineering
DiBlasi Associates
mechanical engineering
AKF
landscape architect
Brown Sardina

client
China World Trade Center Company
Limited
design partner
Brian Lee
managing partner
Gene Schnair
structural engineering partner
Mark Sarkisian
senior designer
Patrick Daly
architectural team
Eric Keune,Terry Meurk, Christiana
Kyrillou, Laith Sayigh, Bennett Shen,
Kirsten Annexstad, James Yan, Peter
Jackson, Andy Ho, Ian Atkins, Tyrone
Marshall
structural team
Neville Mathias, Aaron Mazeika,
Sam Mengelkoch

design director
Nic Jacobs
managing director
Mark Regulinski
senior designers
Peter Lill
team
Davin Benning, Rick Derksen, Rohan
Thotabaduge, Burkhard Musselmann,
Charles Piggott, Micah Chung, Richard
Haigh
project manager
Graham Wiseman
technical coordinator
Martin Miesowicz
mechanical engineering
Luis Malheiro da Silva
structural engineering
Robert Sinn, PE, SE
landscape architect
Fadigas & Associates

Visitor Center
Washington Monument
Washington, D.C.
Designed 2002

client
Grunley-Walsh Construction, National
Park Service
landscape architect
Diana Balmori Associates
design partners
Gary Haney with David M. Childs
senior designers
Rod Garrett, Darrell Puffer
team
Kim Van Holsbeke, Magd Fahmy, Takuya
Yamauchi, Mike Pennington
structural engineering
Thornton Tomasetti Cutts LLC
geotechnical engineering
Muser Rutledge

Image Credits

Introduction
Jock Pottle/ESTO: ill. 3
Ezra Stoller/ESTO: ill. 8, 9

Jury Transcript
K+D Lab: ill. 1
Philip Brown: ill. 2, 5, 6
Jock Pottle/ESTO: ill. 3
Panto Ulema: ill. 8

Project Update Changi Airport
K+D Lab: ill. 1

Automated People Mover Station
Y. Futagawa & Associated
Photographers: context image

Central Plant Building
Keyhole, Inc.: context image
Philip Brown: ill. 4, 9, 13
Jerry Ratto: ill. 2

Concert Hall Lincoln Center
Philip Brown: ill. 11, 20

Deerfield Academy
National Aerial Photography Program:
context image

Greenwich Academy
Florian Holzherr: ill. 5, 10, 11, 15, 16, 17,
18, 19

Mixed-use Tower
Philip Brown: ill. 10, 13

Private Residence / Jordan House
TerraServer.com: context image

Visitor's Center Washington Monument
National Aerial Photography Program:
context image
Eric Schuldenfrei: ill. 13

Bruce Graham Interview
Hedrich-Blessing: ill. 2, 9, 13,
Ezra Stoller/ESTO: ill. 3, 5, 6, 7, 16
Timothy Hursley: ill. 8
James Morris: ill. 21
John Davies: ill. 22

All images courtesy of SOM unless otherwise noted.

We have made every effort to find all
copyright holders. However, should we
have omitted to contact copyright holders
in any individual instances, we would be
most grateful if these copyright holders
would inform us forthwith.

Acknowledgment

The Partners of SOM extend their thanks to all those who contributed to the represented work. We would also like to thank Ross Wimer, Scott Duncan, Simon Frommenwiler, Nicole Robertson, and Kim Sebek for assembling, writing, and coordinating the materials for this Journal 2. In addition we would like to thank Marshall Strabala and Doris Pulsifer for organizing and conducting the Jury Meeting.

Edited by
Wilfried Wang

Copyediting
Tas Skorupa

Design and Typesetting
SOM with Stefanie Langner

Reproduction
Franz Kaufmann GmbH,
Ostfildern-Ruit

Printed by
Dr. Cantz'sche Druckerei,
Ostfildern-Ruit

Published by
Hatje Cantz Verlag
Senefelderstrasse 12
73760 Ostfildern-Ruit
Germany
Tel. +49 / 711 / 4 40 50
Fax +49 / 711 / 4 40 52 20
www.hatjecantz.de

Distribution in the US
D.A.P., Distributed Art Publishers, Inc.
155 Avenue of the Americas,
Second Floor
New York, N.Y. 10013-1507
Tel. +1 / 212 / 627 1999
Fax +1 / 212 / 627 9484

ISBN 3-7757-1266-6

Printed in Germany